Dedication

To our children,
Elizabeth, Channing, Setse, Victoria, and Inle
May you know the joys of extraordinary love
and may you nurture it with happiness habits every day

Praise for *75 Habits for a Happy Marriage*

"If you've lost that loving feeling, *75 Habits for a Happy Marriage* should top your to-do list. This book offers a wealth of small steps you can take to bring the warmth and romance back into your marriage. The advice is both wise and practical. I especially love the concrete ideas for what to do on a date to make it a success. Highly recommended!"

—*Claire Hatch, LCSW, author of* Save Your Marriage: Get Rid of Your Resentment

"Ashley and Daniel Bush bring an enlightened insight to couples. This book gives you helpful, effective methods to foster positive mind-brain-body changes. You can reawaken your love by forging healthy habits in connection, communication, and intimacy. In addition, this book will teach you to value what you have and guide you to reclaim your positive feelings. The bulk of the book gives clear exercises for implementing habits that will change how you think and feel in yourself and about each other. And with inspiring stories and a warm and easy style, you will find the habits easy to implement. Do the exercises, and you will naturally and gently discover the joys that a close and happy relationship can bring!"

—*C. Alexander Simpkins, PhD, and Annellen M. Simpkins, PhD, authors of*
Zen Meditation in Psychotherapy *and* The Dao of Neuroscience

"Here's a perfect resource for couples, exploring daily attitudes and behaviors so central to building and maintaining joy and intimacy. While so many other marriage guides focus on damage control, this book is instead a veritable treasure trove of small, practical steps any couple can regularly take to avoid toxic 'drift,' and to nurture a happy partnership. As a couples therapist, I will wholeheartedly recommend this 'marital mindfulness' gem to my clients!"

—*Susan Lager, LCSW, author of* The Couplespeak™ Series:
"I'm Talking! Are You Listening?" Fix Communication Problems with Your Partner in No Time Flat! *and* Become Relationship Smart Without a Lifetime of Therapy

"Whether newlywed, happily married for many years, or somewhere in between, *75 Habits for a Happy Marriage* will offer a breath of fresh air and new energy to your relationship. It reminds us that now is the time to build intimacy, boost sensuality, and offer gratitude."

—*Judy Ringer, author of* Unlikely Teachers: Finding the Hidden Gifts in Daily Conflict

75 HABITS

FOR A

Marriage
Advice to
Recharge
and

HAPPY

Reconnect
Every Day

MARRIAGE

ASHLEY DAVIS BUSH, LCSW
—— AND ——
DANIEL ARTHUR BUSH, PhD

Avon, Massachusetts

Published by
Adams Media, a division of F+W Media, Inc.
57 Littlefield Street, Avon, MA 02322. U.S.A.
www.adamsmedia.com

ISBN 10: 1-4405-6225-3
ISBN 13: 978-1-4405-6225-9
eISBN 10: 1-4405-6226-1
eISBN 13: 978-1-4405-6226-6

Printed in the United States of America.

10 9 8 7 6 5 4 3 2 1

Many of the designations used by manufacturers and sellers to distinguish their product are claimed as trademarks. Where those designations appear in this book and F+W Media was aware of a trademark claim, the designations have been printed with initial capital letters.

This book is available at quantity discounts for bulk purchases.
For information, please call 1-800-289-0963.

Contents

PART IV: INTIMACY-BUILDING HABITS 133

Introduction

Imagine being together with the one you love without negativity. Imagine a rich, loving relationship built on the foundations of kindness, appreciation, compliments, affection, support, honesty, tenderness, and attention. Imagine experiencing these fulfilling qualities on a daily basis.

The key to a great marriage is the quality of the habits you share together. Healthy, positive habits create an extraordinarily happy marriage. Negative habits create chronic dissatisfaction.

Fortunately, healthy habits can be learned. This book will help you learn and integrate them into your daily life. You can read the chapters from start to finish or simply choose one habit at a time from whichever section interests you the most. The four parts of this book include the following:

Part I, "The Fundamentals," offering a thorough grounding in the essential elements of understanding extraordinary love and the nature of habits.

Part II, "Connection-Building Habits," offering two chapters of habits that are useful on a daily basis to help you connect emotionally and physically.

Part III, "Communication-Building Habits," offering two chapters of habits to help you talk to each other when you're out on a date and when you're experiencing conflict (which is inevitable, by the way).

Part IV, "Intimacy-Building Habits," offering three chapters of habits that focus on the senses, heart, and spirit as gateways to taking your relationship to a new dimension, both deeper and higher.

We know that these habits work for couples because they are based on cutting-edge marriage counseling techniques, mindfulness science, energy medicine, positive psychology, neuroscience, attachment theory, spiritual principles, and common sense.

Each of the 75 happiness habits is triggered by an ordinary "prompt" in your life, such as "when you're eating dinner" or "when you're watching TV together." You'll find that the habits take almost no time to absorb into full and busy lifestyles. Adopting even a handful of them will make a huge impact on your marriage.

Each habit is also illustrated with an anecdote, either personal or clinical. All client names and identifying characteristics have been changed in order to protect privacy. Many of the stories are composites based on Ashley's twenty-five years of clinical experience. Any specific case or situation that you may recognize is purely coincidental.

This book is generally written in the first person based on my (Ashley's) long career as a therapist, but it is very much a mutual collaboration. Daniel is not only a vigilant editor and contributor but has also developed, tested, and continues to live the habits with me. This book simply wouldn't have been possible without both of us.

Daniel and I have been fortunate to experience a wonderfully rich and healing love together. Our marriage sustains and enriches us both individually and jointly. However, we know that we can't take our relationship for granted. Even a wondrous love will wilt away if it is riddled with habits of neglect or abuse. Our marriage is only as strong as the happiness habits that we cultivate every day.

If you long for a deeper connection with your mate—if you crave more intimacy on a daily basis—then these habits are for you. Read. Learn. Practice. You deserve to be deliriously happy in your marriage. And with these tools, you can be.

PART I

The Fundamentals

If you were asked to define what constitutes a happy marriage, you might be puzzled for a minute. It's sometimes easier to recognize one than to actually explain what it consists of. We all know couples who are happily married . . . and probably know marriages that careen from crisis to crisis or that stagnate into a sullen partnership without passion or even love.

But what do we really *mean* when we say two people have a happy marriage?

One thing we don't mean is just that they've been together a long time. (A client once told me that she was glad her husband of fifty-three years had died, since she'd been miserable for the past half century.) A *long* marriage does not necessarily equal a *happy* marriage. And yet, we almost always assume they are synonymous. A silver anniversary, a golden anniversary—we usually take these benchmarks as great accomplishments, rare achievements in a society littered with the corpses of failed marriages. But the truth is that a long marriage is only that—long. It just means that two people have stayed legally bound for a lot of years—maybe joyfully, maybe miserably, or maybe both.

A happy marriage, however, has a certain effervescence as well as a quality of emotional sanctuary that makes your world a better place.

This section looks at the fundamentals of what actually creates such a happy union (Chapter 1) and the habits necessary to keep that happiness in place (Chapter 2).

CHAPTER 1

Extraordinary Love

Ahhh, I love weddings. Big or small, elaborate or simple—they are so full of hope and the promise of love. To find someone and make both a personal and public commitment to join your lives together—what an amazement!

During the early stage of a relationship, you are intoxicated with intimacy. You think about your beloved eagerly. You cannot wait to see if he or she called, e-mailed, or texted. You fantasize about him or her during the day and happily spend nights and weekends together because there's nowhere else you'd rather be. It's as if a protective bubble surrounds you in a private loving world. In this "couple bubble," you dwell effortlessly every day. Focusing on your beloved is so natural and spontaneous that you hardly think about it.

Every couple has a "falling in love" story, a time when the relationship felt fresh and exciting. When a couple comes to see me for counseling, although they are eager to tell me everything that is going wrong in their relationship (or everything that's wrong with their *spouse*), I am particularly interested to know about their courtship. What drew them to each other? How did they behave when they were falling in love? Can they tell me the story of their early time together with a twinkle in their eyes?

Daniel and I first met in Emerald City in the land of Oz; it was literally "magical." I was Glinda the Good Witch and he was on the tech crew in a community theater production of *The Wizard of Oz*. I'll never forget when I first laid eyes on him. He was up above the stage, leaning over a gaping hole thirty feet above, looking down. I was sitting in the front row of the theater when I looked up and our eyes locked. He broke into a huge, Cheshire cat grin as he looked down at me. I believe that I blushed. *What is he smiling about?* I thought. That smile was a foreshadowing of a great love soon to be discovered.

So Happy Together

But of course for all couples, the falling-in-love euphoria fueled by a steady dose of feel-good hormones (oxytocin and dopamine) eventually starts to wear off (generally after a period from six months to two years). What happens when love settles down into real life? Are you doomed to a stale, pale version of the initial brightness?

Many people live as if that's true. In fact, I venture to say that a majority of people in monogamous relationships (whether young, old, childless, with children, remarried, gay, or straight) live in varying degrees of unhappiness.

There's the angry couple and the sexless couple, the couple leading parallel lives and the couple stuck in quiet desperation. There are couples locked in patterns of dysfunction and others reluctantly resigned to living as roommates.

Perhaps a client of mine summed it up best when, during my first session with her, I asked her to describe her relationship with her husband. "It is what it is," she stated matter-of-factly.

"Are you happy in your marriage?" I probed.

She said flatly, "Happy marriages are a myth, a fairy tale. I learned that a long time ago."

That was her experience. But it doesn't have to be yours. In fact, Daniel and I decided to write this book because we feel so deeply that most couples can be happier than they currently are.

Love doesn't have to diminish after the dopamine wears off. Love is like a fine red wine: It actually improves—or rather has the *potential* to improve—over time. This happens because two people have the opportunity to grow together, heal each other, and awaken themselves to life in a new way.

This may sound rather grand—and it is. But two people who love each other create an energy between them that becomes greater than the sum of their parts. The initial "you" and "me" becomes a "we." This third entity, the loving relationship, if well tended, can lead to a rich happiness.

Happily coupled people are healthier and live longer. They laugh more. They experience life as sweeter, joy as deeper, and their love spills over to the world. We have discovered this rich way of living and we want you to as well.

The Three Components of Love

Love may be hard to define but there are three components that are essential to making love extraordinary: connection, communication, and intimacy.

1. *Connection*—feeling close to your lover, bonded, united in your approach to life; often having shared interests and values; a sense of being linked that goes beyond this world; caring about your mate's needs as well as your own; collaboration and compromise.
2. *Communication*—being able to talk freely, being honest with each other, sharing from the heart; a sense of hearing and being heard, understanding and being understood; showing mutual respect and consideration to each other.
3. *Intimacy*—being "naked" (physically, emotionally, spiritually); sharing yourself in your vulnerable, unmasked tenderness; transparency about who you really are and being accepted as such; mutual unveiling; authenticity and openheartedness; a powerful sense of safety and trust.

Each of these three relationship essentials is a building block of your new partnership when you're falling in love, and they actually can get stronger over time. As the years go by, successful couples make them the rock-solid foundation of a happy marriage.

Reverse Direction

But let's say that these qualities have not been deepening for you through the years. Perhaps the threads of connection, communication, and intimacy that you wove during your courtship have come undone. Perhaps the strands are fraying and your carpet is threadbare.

It's time to take stock and turn things around ... reverse direction before it's too late. Daniel and I both know that sometimes a relationship will come unraveled. Both of us in our first marriages, (each of which lasted seventeen years), had let connection, communication, and intimacy crumble. For myself, I resented the growing distance between me and my first husband, but my attempts to reach out came across as nagging and attacking. I chalked up the growing divide between us to lives that were too busy. *One day it will get better, I thought.* But one day never came. At some point, I lost the motivation to even attempt a repair.

Sex, Money, and Kids

What causes the stresses and strains that, if not addressed, can tear a marriage apart? Most researchers would agree that there are three big sources of tension among married couples.

1. *Sex*—Sometimes there's too little of it; sometimes too much. Sometimes the couples aren't aligned to one another's sexual needs and interests. And sometimes it's just a big elephant sitting in the relationship's living room, waiting for somebody to notice it.
2. *Money*—Money—or a lack of money—puts an extra strain on married couples. When you're worried about money, it shows up in other parts of your relationship. Usually that worry finds the weakest part of the relationship and beats on it until it breaks.
3. *Kids*—As we'll talk about elsewhere, having kids is magical. It's also difficult. You have to make so many life-changing decisions about how to raise them. Naturally, couples fight about this.

In the twenty-first century, there is a heavy pull of life on the couple. Most relationships stand in line behind the demands of a career, children, hobbies, chores, and extended family. It's as if there's a conspiracy in modern living that actually de-prioritizes the primary couple relationship. Everywhere are the surface demands of life, the superficialities that comprise your waking hours: Pay your bills, get to work on time, respond to that e-mail, return that phone call, sign the form for the teacher, mow the lawn, clean the house, buy the groceries, service the car, feed the cats, prepare meals, floss your teeth—need I go on?

Then there are the gadgets that, more often than not, draw you away from your beloved: smartphones, laptops, notebooks, netbooks, tablets, iPods. Every year more devices of distraction reveal themselves.

Meanwhile, individuals are richly supported for being workaholics. There is after-school care to accommodate longer work hours, carpool support from neighbors, and year-end bonuses for dedication to work. But how many friends, bosses, or colleagues say, "Stop everything. I'll watch your kids. Go focus on your relationship!" Not many.

Our relentless career focus, extended families, children, hobbies, and the uncompromising pace of modern life erode the essential fabric of intimacy in the primary couple. The "couple bubble" has no sanctuary.

While in the beginning of a relationship the couple bubble is prized and protected, for many couples, the bubble bursts somewhere along the way. The essential "we" becomes vulnerable to the layers of busy lives.

Patterns of Destruction

As if modern living weren't enough to challenge the romantic relationship, as time passes, couples seem to forget how to bring out the best in each other. The once-doting lovers start to take each other for granted, and eventually, they simply ignore each other. Less time together combines with poor quality time together to create a feeling of disconnect.

Couples long to feel intimately connected, yet when individuals are starved for true intimacy they feel frustrated. As a result, they lash out with criticism, blame, and insults. They shut down with awkward, grumpy silences and stop listening to each other. When couples get caught in these patterns of negative interaction and benign neglect, it only increases their despair.

Eventually one or both partners look outside the marriage to have their intimacy needs fulfilled. Typical outlets for this are an extramarital affair, obsessive ambition, hyper-involved parenting, or consuming obsession with a hobby.

Being unhappy and lonely within a relationship is extremely painful. Feeling as if you don't matter to your partner has a way of activating a primal panic. Whether suffering from being ignored or hurting from a verbal assault, the pain of rejection cuts to the core.

Two Sides of the Same Coin

I have an interesting perspective in my work. As a couples therapist, I see highly distressed couples who are unhappy with their relationships and are longing for love. Meanwhile, as a grief counselor, I see highly distressed mourners who *were* extremely happy with their relationships and are longing for that lost love.

Working with grievers for more than twenty-five years has given me a unique vantage point. I have heard so many heartbreaking stories of loss: the stunned widow whose thirty-six-year-old husband dropped dead at work, leaving her to raise three children under the age of five; the bereft widow whose husband passed away in his sleep just two weeks shy of their much-anticipated mutual retirement; the inconsolable widower who couldn't imagine living after his sweetheart of forty-five years lost her battle with cancer.

It is never easy to lose your beloved, whether you have been together for two years or twenty. When you do find yourself at his or her funeral, all you can think is that you wished you had a little bit more time together. All you want is one more hug, one more kiss, one more night beside your dear one.

The lesson from loss is clear: You must dedicate yourself to loving habits each day because each day may be the last that you have together.

In Sickness and in Health

Of course it's one thing to know the preciousness of life in your head and it's another to know its value deep in your heart—to feel it all the way to your gut. Brushing up close against mortality has a way of highlighting what is most important.

A few years into our marriage, Daniel was diagnosed with colon cancer. I remember hearing the words "the biopsy is cancerous." Dan was in his training as a mental-health counselor. We were in the midst of rehearsals for a community theater production of *Fiddler on the Roof*. We were starting to work on this book together. We were in the middle of life; how could this happen?

Everything on the to-do list got shelved as we dealt with a new world of doctor visits, medical tests, surgery, recovery, and eventually chemotherapy. I watched my stunningly handsome husband fight for his life, becoming increasingly frail and wan.

Before his diagnosis, he was a strapping man at 6' 5", weighing a hefty 230 pounds. By his ninth round of chemo, he was a shadow of himself, having lost nearly 50 pounds. And on the bad days (of which there were many), he could hardly lift his head off the pillow. My superman, my boundlessly energetic "go to" guy, was gone.

I felt a kinship with the thousands of men and women who watch their beloved mates decline in body and mind through the ravages of cancer, assorted illnesses, Alzheimer's, and dementia. And I'm one of the lucky ones because he has since recovered.

Still, I got a preview, a reminder that our lives will end, one way or another, sooner or later. There is no time to waste.

Stars Aligned

Of all the billions of people on this planet, you and your beloved crossed paths at a single moment in time. The stars aligned in the universe, and you found each other. You met, fell in love, and made a decision to be together. For some reason, for some purpose, your lives are linked.

Extraordinary love doesn't mean that every day is a honeymoon. Certainly there will be ebbs of closeness and even flows of distance in your many marriages within your marriage. Each stage in your life together—having a new baby, burying a parent, illness, empty nest, retirement—will be cause for you to re-evaluate your relationship and regroup as a couple.

But if you make the deep current of your relationship about soul-to-soul growth and intoxicating union, then your life will be unbelievably rich. Consider it a gift to each other to make your relationship as vibrant as it can possibly be . . . this day and every day.

CHAPTER 2

Happiness Habits

What's a habit? It's something you do regularly, something that becomes, after a while, almost unconscious. Think about some of the habits you already have: for example, your morning routine. You get out of bed and proceed through a series of mindless tasks: Make your bed, use the bathroom, brush your teeth, take a shower, get dressed, eat breakfast. These are habits you learned, many of them when you were a child, some of them later in life. By sheer practice, they've become automatic. They help get your day off to the right start.

It's quite possible as well that you've got some bad habits. For instance, maybe you check your e-mails first thing in the morning rather than take a moment to center yourself. Or perhaps you eat a pastry every morning rather than a nutritious breakfast.

The habits for a healthy, happy marriage aren't fundamentally different from other kinds of habits. They've got to be learned and practiced. Sometimes, in doing that, you've got to break bad habits that are injuring your relationship. Let's look at an example.

Bad Marriage Habits

Mary and Bob have unhealthy relationship habits. They've been married for fifteen years and, truth be told, don't think too hard about their marriage. If you asked Mary if she felt close to Bob, she would say he's like a comfortable shoe—worn and familiar. If you asked her if there was spice to their connection, she would say that spice is unrealistic after the first year of courtship.

If you asked Bob if he felt intimate with Mary he would say, "I guess, sure." He might assume that all was well as long as Mary wasn't complaining and as long as they had sex fairly regularly.

However, both Mary and Bob feel lonely, underappreciated, and stressed. They can't quite pinpoint why because life appears relatively good: They're healthy, their kids are doing fine, they each have jobs, and they share a nice home. And yet, there is a chronic underlying sense of dissatisfaction.

A typical weekday for Mary and Bob includes early-morning departures to full-time jobs, no communication until 3 P.M., Mary running kids to activities into the early evening, Bob coming home late from work and giving Mary a peck on the cheek, Mary complaining that he doesn't help around the house, Bob feeling nagged, Mary folding clothes before going to bed without Bob, Bob staying up late to watch TV or work in the basement. Both of them end the day feeling lonely and unsupported.

Mary and Bob have sex about every other month or so. They go out to dinner together about four times a year. They see family and friends on weekends but rarely spend time alone together. Notably, they don't have conversations with each other about the state of their relationship.

Poor Mary and Bob. They're caught on the treadmill, the relentless pace of modern society that threatens to squeeze the joy out of living. Because of their bad relationship habits, they are asleep to the miracles in their midst.

It is likely that eventually one of them will encounter the potential for intimacy outside the marriage, maybe with a friend or colleague (which may or may not end the marriage). Or maybe Bob and Mary will simply numb out their intimacy needs, losing themselves in obsessive work, family activities, excessive drinking, shopping, or Internet use until one day, after the kids are grown, they'll wonder, "Who is this stranger in my bed?" (if they even still share a bed). They will end their days feeling lonely and deadened inside.

And yet, there was a time when Mary and Bob were crazy about each other. They were so in love, in fact, that they willingly joined their lives. They chose to build a life together, have a family, and grow old side by side. But somehow, through the years, they lost sight of the intimacy that was the initial foundation of that hopeful beginning.

A Foundation of Healthy Habits

Habits—whether healthy or otherwise—create neural pathways or "grooves" in your brain. You want a brain grooved for emotional safety, compassion, and joyful connection. Repetitive healthy habits are the way to get this. Love might be the reason you got married, but a brain wired for intimacy is what will sustain your marriage over the long haul.

When Daniel and I began to live together, I thought at first that our great love would sustain us, and that keeping our intimate connection would be a breeze. But who was I kidding?

Nobody tells you how complicated a second marriage can be—or at least nobody told me. The love of my life was a package deal. He came with two children, an ex-wife, the ex's new partner, that partner's children, the ex-in-laws, and the usual assortment of ordinary in-laws.

I, too, was hardly an island. With three children, an ex-husband, his new partner, my ex-in-laws, and the usual assortment of extended family plus pets, I was more of an archipelago. Add to this a non-overlapping joint custody arrangement tracked by a six-month wall calendar that resembled air-traffic control, and life became complex and full indeed.

It was immediately apparent to me that regular healthy habits were our only hope of keeping a strong foundation for our marriage. Without them, we would be swept away in an avalanche of life.

Can small moments of daily intimacy really make that much of a difference? Yes! While traditionally recommended intimacy activities—such as weekends away, vacations, weekly sex, and hobbies together—are good for the health of your relationship, they are not enough. Without healthy habits practiced *every single day*, your relationship will suffer.

We know that the happiness habits in this book will help you feel closer every day, and we know because we use them! Their effectiveness is based on tried and true foundations.

- Emotionally Focused Couples Therapy (EFT)—This framework emphasizes attachment theory and the need to create a secure bonding attachment between partners.
- Imago Relationship Therapy—This framework emphasizes listening/ mirroring skills and a need to understand how to help each other heal childhood wounds.
- The Five Love Languages—This framework looks at how different people express love and prefer to receive love based on the following modes: touch, verbal affirmation, acts of service, quality time, and gifts.
- Couples research—John Gottman is a pioneer in couples research and can predict with 97 percent accuracy which couples will divorce based on whether they fall prey to the four "horsemen" (criticism, contempt, defensiveness, and stonewalling).
- Neuroplasticity and rewiring the brain—Current neuroscientific research confirms that we can change neural pathways in the brain for the better by having repeated and sustained positive experiences.
- Mindfulness-based therapies—Mindfulness brings an attitude of curiosity, receptivity, and nonjudgmental awareness to present experience. Being in the moment leads to compassion and less emotional reactivity.
- Positive psychology and gratitude—Gratitude practices lead to higher levels of happiness, life satisfaction, and overall well-being. Most couples chronically underappreciate each other.
- Energy medicine and bodywork—Energy medicine integrates the body's energy (electromagnetic fields) and the manipulation of that energy via touch. Bodywork of all kinds is a powerful form of nonverbal communication that links mind, body, and spirit.

I have seen happy couples become happier as they integrate these happiness habits into their daily routine, and I have seen distressed couples turn their relationship around as they work with these habits in their lives.

At the Core

Each of the habits in this book creates an intentional break in the automated and seemingly relentless pace of life. They initiate a "pattern interrupt" to the usual stream of behaviors, thoughts, and reactions. In that space of purposeful interruption, the habit becomes a moment of intimate connection. Who among us doesn't want more of that?

Essential to each habit is brevity: short and simple. If a new activity together is too time-consuming, labor-intensive, or expensive (such as taking up golf), it is less likely to happen. But easy suggestions, like "touch your mate during dinner" or "have a twenty-second hug at the end of the day," are doable on a daily basis.

The strategy here is to avoid the "New Year's Resolution Syndrome." It's easy to make a big proclamation about how everything is going to be different on January 1. But sadly, as you know, few resolutions are ever kept. By Valentine's Day most are a distant memory.

The key to lasting change in your relationship (or any goal, for that matter) is to integrate bite-sized, practical changes into your daily routine. Over time, the wonder of a close relationship will become your reality. The beauty of couples' happiness habits is that they set you up for success!

Frequently Asked Questions

Having worked with many couples over the years, I've learned to expect certain questions. Here are a few of the queries that come up most often, along with our answers.

What if my partner won't participate? Can I do this alone?

The answer is a resounding "Yes!" You are part of a dynamic duo. As you begin to make changes in your patterns, the entire relationship system will be affected. It may take two to tango, but it only takes one to redirect the dance.

Try several new habits consistently for a few weeks and see how your mate responds.

Why should I be the nice one when my spouse is so neglectful or rude?
Because you shouldn't let your partner determine your level of consciousness. By consciousness, I mean your ability to respond with generosity, compassion, kindness, and love.

It's easy to point your finger toward your partner and notice all the ways that he or she falls short, fails, and doesn't meet your needs. But consider turning that finger around and pointing to yourself. Are you the kind of partner that *you* would want? How do *you* rate as a partner? Would you say, "I do," to yourself? Do you meet your partner's needs?

Be the partner that you would desire. If you raise the bar on behaviors that are thoughtful, warm, kind, and loving, chances are high that your mate will begin to respond.

What if I don't feel like being loving?
Then "fake it 'til you make it." Neuroscience has demonstrated that our feelings and our behaviors are connected. Just as changes in how you feel lead to changes in how you behave, so do changes in how you behave lead to changes in how you feel. That holds true for being nice, for behaving affectionately, and even for making love.

How quickly will these habits take to work?
The habits help you feel connected immediately. However, it takes about twenty-one days of consecutive use for a habit to stick. So it's best to try a few habits and see which ones you want to use regularly. Then commit to integrating them into your life for twenty-one days. Hint: It's easy to forget the habits until they become second nature, so use Post-it notes or digital reminders as prompts for yourself!

What if I find that I only use the habits sporadically?

Using the tools a little bit is better than not using them at all. You may find that you start using a tool and then forget it or switch to other tools. Don't get discouraged if you let the habit slip. It takes time and awareness to create new patterns in your marriage. Any day is a good day to start—or restart—a new habit.

Aren't relationships, in the end, just a lot of hard work?

This perspective always amuses me because it makes love seem like such a drudgery, a chore, with all the sex appeal of cleaning toilets. Who wants more "work" in a world where we practically work 24/7 as it is?

No, relationships require nourishment, that's all. Healthy habits are nourishment for a happy marriage. Think of your body: You can have plenty of unhealthy habits that will lead to heart disease, high cholesterol, and obesity. Or you can have healthy habits that make you feel alive and vibrant. Feed your relationship with unhealthy habits and you might end up in divorce court. But use the healthy habits in this book and together you'll feel like a million bucks.

PART II

Connection-Building Habits

They sat in front of me like nervous school children with their heads lowered. They cleared their throats and shuffled their feet. He began to gaze at the books on my bookshelf. I asked them why they had come to see me.

Deborah said, "I can't communicate with him. I think we have a big communication problem. He doesn't hear me."

"And do you think you have a communication problem?" I asked Stan.

"No," Stan replied. "I'm pretty happy actually. I think she's making a big deal out of nothing."

Hmmm.

"Can you tell me what a typical evening is like in your home?" I asked.

Stan said, "Well, when I come home from work, I'm pretty tired. We eat dinner while we watch the news. Then, I check sports stats on the computer. She puts our five-year-old, Paula, to sleep. I don't really have energy for much else."

Deborah interjected: "He never even seems excited to see me—or Paula for that matter. I can't get his attention. He doesn't listen to me—his eyes just glaze over even though I have stuff to tell him. And then he goes to the computer and that's it for the night."

I sat back and said to them both, "I think what you really have is a *connection* problem."

While almost every couple I ever work with at some point tell me that they have trouble communicating, often what they mean is that they have trouble connecting. Connection is a feeling of powerful closeness. It generates the energy of togetherness as you go through life. From that place, communication evolves naturally.

This section of the book offers a specific selection of core connection-building habits (Chapter 3) and habits of physical affection (Chapter 4). Both will deepen and enrich your relationship.

Your Daily Thread: Habits to Weave Through Your Day

If your relationship were a plant, what condition would you say describes it? Dry? Blooming? Wilted? Robust?

Like a plant, your relationship needs regular tender loving care. It needs the soil of everyday connection, the nutrients of focused attention, and the sunlight of love. Watering your plant once or twice a year won't suffice. Giving it sunlight every month or two isn't enough either. Your plant needs nourishment every single day.

Fortunately, each day offers a wealth of transitional moments that are perfect opportunities for building habits that nourish your relationship and help feelings of connection and intimacy take root.

The key transitional moments in your day, as couples therapists have known for years, are the "launches" and the "landings" (how you separate for the day and how you reunite at the end of a day). But transition moments are happening all day long, and each one offers an opportunity to build healthy habits that keep yourself and your relationship nourished.

Use the daily habits in this chapter to build core connection skills so that you can soak up the warmth of intimacy throughout the day. They are organized chronologically from your first waking moment until your final goodnight.

Good Morning, Sunshine

PROMPT: Every day when you wake up, before you get out of bed in the morning

HABIT: Lie on your back and place one hand on your heart. Place the other hand on your lower belly. Rest like this for a minute and imagine you're radiating a brilliant light. Breathe in the word "Love" (light shining on you) and breathe out the word "Love" (light radiating from you). Feel tenderness and compassion for *you*, as well as for your partner.

PURPOSE: The physical pose of this tool (hand on heart, hand on belly) mimics the comforting stance of an infant being held. When a baby is held by an adult, the entire length of his or her little body is cradled in the warmth of the grownup's body. When you put pressure on those key points, you recreate a primal soothing feeling.

This habit also speaks to an important issue: self-compassion. When you have a daily grounding in self-love and self-compassion, you set the stage to improve your marriage. It is hard to give something you don't have. Fill up your own tank with self-love every morning, and there will be plenty to share.

Twenty-nine-year-old Sarah had tears in her eyes. She and her husband were in a new marriage after a whirlwind courtship. But something was off track. She had come to see me because she felt that her low self-esteem was interfering with her relationship. She put her head down and sighed as she proclaimed, "I'm so stupid; I'm such an idiot really. I don't know how Hugo can love me because I don't even love myself. I don't even *like* myself."

Hugo had told her that her constant negative self-talk was a turnoff. Sarah said, "I know that he just wants me to be happy and feel good about myself."

Clearly it wasn't going to be enough to tell Sarah—or ask Hugo to tell her—that she was a wonderful, warm person with a lot of love to give. She had to get in the habit of feeling good about herself. I instructed her to start working with the "Good Morning, Sunshine" exercise and to continue with it until it became an ingrained part of her morning routine. She was willing but skeptical. She told me that even if she said the word "Love," she wouldn't feel it.

"That's okay," I assured her. "Just stay with breathing in the word and the light of 'Love.'" Reluctantly, she agreed.

The next week she told me that the tool hadn't worked. She said that when she put her hand on her lower belly, it disgusted her. "The only thing I could think about was how fat and fleshy my stomach felt. I'm sure Hugo must feel that way too, whenever he touches me."

So many women are at war with their bodies. I suggested she keep both hands on her chest until she developed more tenderness toward her body. Most important, I reiterated that this exercise had to become a habit. She agreed to keep using the tool every day for twenty-one days. "We'll see how you feel then," I told her.

Sarah used the tool and reported to me that sometimes she got tearful when she breathed in the word "Love." But as she continued to direct that love, that tenderness toward herself, she felt something inside her shifting. After the third week of consistent use, she beamed as she told me, "I can put my hand on my tummy now. It's just another part of me. I think I'm making progress. You know, maybe I'm not so bad after all."

"That's great," I said. "How is that affecting things with Hugo?"

Sarah's smile turned gentle. "I'm not talking about myself in such a bad way. I can tell that makes him happy. Now that I'm not getting in my own way, I notice that I'm a lot better at telling Hugo all the things I love about him."

REFLECTION: How do you interact differently with your spouse when you begin your day by loving yourself?

HABIT 2

First Light

PROMPT: When you first wake up in the morning—or when your partner wakes up

HABIT: Establish a loving connection by saying to your spouse, "I love being married to you"—or words of your choosing. The exact words you use aren't important; what's essential is to convey a message that your partner is special to you ("You matter to me," "You're the best thing that ever happened to me," or "I'm glad we're going through life together."). Say this in person if possible. If, for some reason, you're not there, text it, e-mail it, leave a phone message, or stick a note to the refrigerator. An important element of this habit is to vary both the message and the way you deliver it. Continue to find new ways to verbally express your love until this becomes a natural part of your morning routine.

PURPOSE: How you greet your spouse in the morning sets the tone for the day. Couples therapist gurus, Gay and Kathlyn Hendricks, authors of *Conscious Loving* and founders of the Hendricks Institute, teach the importance of the first daily communication. Gay has said that when he first sees Katie in the morning, he makes sure to tell her that she's the most special person in the universe. *Wow!* No wonder they've been happily married for more than three decades.

In my first marriage, silence greeted me in the mornings. With a long commute ahead of him, my husband woke up hours before me. We agreed that he would sneak out without waking me.

In fact, we routinely had no interaction for the entire day. He told me that it was hard to touch base because he was so busy. In those days, texting didn't exist, nor did we think to use e-mail. Usually he would call around 5 P.M. on his way home from work (this often being our first conversation of the day) at which time the subject matter was usually, "What's for dinner?" There's nothing intrinsically wrong with having large gaps of noncommunication. However, the lack of early-day intimacy, coupled with a growing overall deficit of attention and appreciation created the emotional distance that ultimately led to the breakdown of our marriage.

In my second marriage, we are more intentional about our first communication. Daniel is the earlier riser on most mornings . . . and he is often the first to offer kisses and words of love. When he departs early, he leaves me a love note. However, I know that this habit is also an important practice for me personally in order to keep my heart open. Therefore, before my day gets started, I'll offer him some loving words as well. If I need inspiration, I will often think, "What would Gay say?"

REFLECTION: Do you prefer to hear words of adoration in the morning rather than say them? Be the one to set the tone for the day with happiness and love.

HABIT 3

It's Raining Love

PROMPT: When you take a shower

HABIT: Think of someone in your life who loves you, a kind of "benefactor" in your life (in the past, present, or even future), whether he or she is currently on this planet or not. You may even choose a spiritual figure (such as Jesus or Buddha) or a beloved pet. Imagine that person's love raining down upon you. As you stand in the shower, feel her love washing over you and saturating you completely. Let your heart expand as you receive and absorb this abundant love. Drink it into your body. Say or think, "I am showered with love."

PURPOSE: Many people have a deep-seated fear that they are unlovable. They fear being rejected, abandoned, and isolated. As a result, they find their marriages lonely, isolating, and unfulfilling.

Interestingly, the template for the adult primary relationship has its roots in the infant's relationship with the primary caretaker. "Secure attachment" occurs when the infant is consistently cared for with little separation, anxiety, or trauma. However, most people grow up with "insecure attachment." This manifests in a marriage as either "anxious/ambivalent" or "avoidant" attachment styles. Don't get too hung up on this terminology. All you need to know at this point is that "anxious/ambivalent" spouses tend to cling and then, if their needs aren't met, withdraw. "Avoidant" spouses shut down their needs to protect themselves, and thus, also withdraw.

Two withdrawn spouses is a recipe for an unhappy marriage. To prevent this— or to fix it if you feel it's happening in your relationship—you need to actively work to keep your heart buoyant and open. The daily habit of consciously filling yourself with abundant love is an antidote to the unconscious impulse to withdraw. Drenching yourself with such love every morning creates an overflowing, healing supply of love to share with others. Once your "cup runneth over," you will find that love flows freely from you.

Josh and Tracy had been making excellent progress in our counseling. They were talking more honestly, connecting more intentionally, and sharing themselves more intimately. I felt encouraged and looked forward to wrapping up our work together.

But when they came into my office on this day, they both, metaphorically, had their arms crossed. Before they even said a word I sensed a powerful tension between them.

"Did something happen?" I asked.

Josh jumped in. "Tracy just shut down from me. It's like she's on some private island that I can't get to. She won't even talk to me . . . or if she does, she's like some robot."

I looked at Tracy and asked, "What's going on?"

Just as Josh said, she was reserved, withdrawn. I could tell that something had triggered an emotional shutdown. I asked Josh, "When did this start?"

"I just made my plans for my brother's birthday celebration . . ." he started.

Tracy interrupted him: ". . . *without* me."

The story unfolded: Josh was joining his brothers on a fiftieth birthday trip to Las Vegas, and no spouses were invited. One of his brothers had asked for this once-in-a-lifetime brother trip. Unfortunately, the trip triggered an attachment injury for Tracy. Rather than feel happy for her husband, she felt hurt and abandoned, and so she shut down.

In shutting down, she compromised the "us" space of her marriage, creating a wall between them. I suggested the "It's Raining Love" habit as a way not only to get past this crisis but to help her keep her heart open. She reluctantly agreed.

Afterward, I heard from the couple that the habit was successful—so much so that sometimes Josh joins Tracy in the shower just to make sure she's feeling enough love.

REFLECTION: How would your life be different if you focused on the abundance of love that you have to give rather than on what you feel you need?

HABIT 4

So Long, Farewell

PROMPT: When you say goodbye before a parting, however brief

HABIT: Looking into the eyes of the one you love, place your hand over your heart and then move it, palm up, out to him, indicating "you have my heart."

PURPOSE: How you "launch" from your spouse in the morning and how you reunite at the end of the day is extremely critical for a happy marriage. If your launches and landings are brief and insignificant, you will tend to take your marriage for granted. However, a habit of intentional connection will highlight your deep love and commitment to each other.

Saying goodbye doesn't imply you won't see each other again, but it does mean some period of separation, during which you'll be thinking about a lot of other things. A habit of a loving farewell each day can remind you of the importance of your marriage and of your spouse.

Expressing love for one another at each parting becomes a way of holding each other close. It affirms your love's permanence in an impermanent world. Living with the truth of the never-ending flow of time around you enriches your experience of the present moment.

When you adopt the habit of filling each parting with a conscious affirmation of love, you will fill each parting with a tenderness that will carry through the day.

On a chilly January day, everything was humming along as usual. But then, unexpectedly, it began to sleet. Snow and sleet in New England is, of course, never completely unexpected. Nevertheless, we hadn't prepared ourselves for a storm.

Dan was due home by 6 P.M. but I had no way to reach him since his cell phone battery had died. As 6 P.M. became 6:30 P.M. became 7 P.M., I worked myself into a panic. With no way to reach him, I began to let my imagination assume the worst.

Finally, around 8 P.M., Dan called home on a AAA worker's cell phone to tell me he had been in a three-car accident on a local road but that he was fine. I was so relieved to hear he was all right that I began crying on the phone.

Knowing that Dan was on his way home was a cause for celebration. I was also happy to know that we had parted in the morning with intention and intimacy.

REFLECTION: Does awareness of the fragility of life cause you to shrink in fear or does it open your heart to your deepest connection?

HABIT 5

Text Treat

PROMPT: When you are at work and are about to have lunch

HABIT: Text your spouse/partner to let her know that you love her, that you're thinking of her, and/or that you look forward to seeing her. Feel free to be playful and flirtatious—send nothing but sweet nothings.

PURPOSE: Staying connected through the day is a vital habit. The number one place for affairs to germinate is at the office. What starts out as a collegial friendship can easily deepen into an emotional attachment and eventually into a physical affair. But by establishing a habit of regularly communicating loving thoughts to your partner during the workday, you ensure that he or she remains focused on you as the most important person in his or her life.

Most spouses spend their days apart. If you don't get in the habit of expressing your love to each other, you can start to dwell in separate spheres. Keeping connected with at least one daily text helps counteract the sense of living parallel lives.

Sally sat across from me with a smile on her face. The last time I had seen her, some three years previously, she had been overwhelmed by her life. At that time, she had a six-month-old baby as well as three-year-old twins. She had complained of feeling fat and unattractive. And she had felt distant from her husband. Although she had wanted to continue therapy, her life was too chaotic to schedule appointments.

During our final session, I had suggested that she find small ways to stay in touch with her husband during the day. Yes, it can be a challenge to stay close when kids are young and family demands are high, but that's no excuse for putting the relationship on the back burner.

Now, I was amazed to see her looking trim and rested. She had come back for a few sessions to process the death of her beloved grandfather. She said that even though this loss was painful, in general she was extremely happy with her life. I was just about to ask about her husband when Beethoven's Fifth Symphony wafted out of her purse.

"Oh, I'm so sorry about that," she responded. As she moved to silence her cell phone, she glanced at the screen and commented, "Oh, it's a text from Gerry." She emitted a girlish giggle and blushed. "He's so sweet."

"How are things with Gerry?" I asked.

"We stay connected during the day now," she said with a smile. "We love texting."

"I'm so glad," I said.

"What you didn't tell me," she continued, "is that staying connected during the day would keep us connected at night!"

REFLECTION: How do your days and nights flow differently when you know that you and your mate are intentionally bonded together?

Picture This

PROMPT: When you're at work, during a coffee break

HABIT: Look at a photograph of your beloved (on your desk, on your computer, on your phone, in your wallet). As you look at the picture, place your right hand over your heart and breathe deeply. Notice the details and recall the circumstances involved in the photograph: the event, the sweater, the mood, the weather. Remember the love that you have for this special person. Hold this loving feeling in your heart for up to twenty seconds, letting the feeling expand within you.

PURPOSE: When you intentionally summon a positive feeling into your awareness and then heighten and expand that feeling, you begin to create new neural pathways in the brain. Research shows that heightening a feeling for twenty or more seconds turns explicit memory (the recollection of an event) into implicit memory (a felt sense rooted in brain structure).

This tool is an adaptation of Rick Hanson's "Taking in the Good" exercise. Hanson (coauthor with Richard Mendius of *Buddha's Brain: The Practical Neuroscience of Happiness, Love, and Wisdom*) explains that intentionally recalling, re-experiencing, and mentally absorbing an event wires positive neural structures in the brain, making it part of your way of being.

Furthermore, placing your hand over your heart creates an immediate physical feeling of calm and connection.

"You may turn on all portable electronic devices," announced the flight attendant. People around me began turning on their laptops. I returned my attention to the book that I was reading.

The older gentleman beside me pulled out his wallet and began sifting through photographs. I glanced over and saw him smiling as he looked at the picture of himself with his arms around a woman.

He turned to look at me and said, "That's me with my beautiful wife. We've been married for thirty-seven incredibly happy years."

Being a couples therapist, I couldn't resist asking a nosy question: "What's your secret for a happy marriage?"

He smiled and sighed. "Well, let's see . . . what is the secret? For me, you know, I never lose sight of the fact that I'm lucky to be sharing my life with this amazing woman. When I look at this picture, I just experience that truth right here," he said, gesturing to his heart.

"Wow," I murmured, "So you look at her picture when you travel just to remember your love?"

He smiled. "Not just when I travel. I look at this picture—or some picture of her—every day. This is my favorite, for some reason. We were on our twentieth wedding anniversary trip in France."

I pressed him. "You look at her picture *every single day?*"

"Of course," he answered. "I like the feeling I get when I look at it. It reminds me that I'm a lucky son of a bitch . . . pardon my French."

We both smiled.

REFLECTION: Allow yourself a moment to really see your spouse in the picture and feel what it's like to love that special person.

HABIT 7

Puppy Love

PROMPT: When you reunite at the end of the day

HABIT: Greet each other with enthusiasm. Be excited and grateful that your beloved has come home. Stop what you're doing, engage in a full body hug (stomach to stomach), and hold the pose for twenty or more seconds. Feel your bodies relax into each other and say, "I'm so glad you're home." (Feel free to use whatever words and phrases best express your love.) If you're the one coming home, go up to your spouse, engage in the extended hug and say, "I'm so glad to be home."

PURPOSE: This reunion hug will feel unusually long at first. However, it takes twenty seconds to stimulate the flow of oxytocin, the bonding hormone. When you activate the release of this hormone, you start to feel closer and more connected right away.

You might find it initially challenging to make this exercise into a habit, because if you're the one coming home, you will have many demands on your attention (check the mail, check the e-mail, hug the kids, return a phone call). And if you're the one already home, you may feel inconvenienced to drop what you were doing in order to engage in this ritual. Most of us are used to a cursory "welcome home" peck—if that.

However, when you develop the habit of this oxytocin-rich reception, you ignite passion. You increase awareness of how precious your partner is to you, and you break the cycle of dull routine and complacency.

Sally complained that her husband barely noticed her when he came home from work. She looked at me and sniffed, "He happily hugs the kids; he even pats the dog enthusiastically. Me? I barely get a nod." Sally wanted more than anything to know that she mattered to her husband.

I knew how she felt. There had been too many times when Dan came home and I felt invisible. Or worse, times when I came home and greeted good old Hickory, my faithful golden retriever, with real enthusiasm while Dan got a simple "Hi."

It just didn't seem right that upon coming home, I could get down on the floor to rub Hickory's belly whereas to Dan I would just say, "Hey, did you remember to pick up milk?"

Yep, guilty. And so, one crisp autumn afternoon, after reflecting on this unsatisfactory reunion, I decided to turn things around and give Daniel a complete puppy welcome. That evening, rather than wait for him to enter the house, which would be customary, I bounded out the front door, ran to him outside and gave him a big hug.

He naturally attempted to pull back after a second but I held on longer. I held on for dear life. Dan began to laugh and started to hug me back.

At that precise moment, our neighbor across the street appeared at the end of his driveway. This curmudgeonly neighbor, a man whom we had hardly ever seen in three years, barked, "Maybe you'd better take it inside."

And so we did.

REFLECTION: How do *you* feel when you make your partner feel cherished when he or she walks in the door?

HABIT 8

Touch Tone

PROMPT: When you're having dinner together, on an average weeknight

HABIT: This habit has two parts: First, turn off the TV and/or all screens while you're eating. Second, make it a point to touch your spouse during the meal. You can either do this secretly, under the table, or publicly for all to see. You can stroke his arm, hold her hand, touch his foot, stroke her cheek . . . whatever takes your fancy at that moment.

PURPOSE: Just as there are habits for a healthy marriage, some habits are unhealthy. Eating in front of the television regularly is bad for you. You interact less as a couple (and as a family), the TV creates a tone of distraction and intrusion, and you tend to overeat while enjoying your food less. Conversely, the habit of eating without watching a screen creates a climate of focused, undivided attention.

Touch is a vital part of feeling and staying connected. By its nature, touch is an intimate, relationship-building activity. In the early stages of their relationship, couples typically touch more frequently. But as time goes by, they touch each other less and less. Rebuilding this touching habit by having a regular time to touch helps create intimacy and highlights the "us" space.

If you live with children, the dual habits of no TV and intentional touching model for them a sense of tender, focused affection that they will carry into their adult relationships. Dinner time should be a brief respite from the world at large, an opportunity for safe harbor, for refueling after a busy day.

I recently worked with a middle-aged couple with no children whose wife complained that they don't connect at the end of the day. I asked her to describe a typical evening at home.

"We watch the news during dinner," Laura said, "and then Ralph goes to the basement to work on his stuff. I just end up reading in the bedroom. We hardly say a word to each other."

Television during dinner—the kiss of death, I thought. While I'm not generally opposed to news or entertainment programs, I know it's healthier for a couple or family to spend fifteen to thirty minutes screen free while they reconnect over the dinner table.

I gave Laura and Ralph a homework assignment: During the next week, spend each dinner without television and see what happened.

The next week when they came to their session, Laura was delighted to tell me of their progress. It turned out that they actually enjoyed talking to each other without the distraction of the television. For them, mealtime television had simply become a sloppy habit that needed to change.

For homework over the next weekend, I asked them to touch each other several times during dinner. During the next session, Laura and Ralph were both smiling. "Ralph doesn't always go to the basement anymore," she said, grinning. "I guess he discovered that reading in bed with me isn't so bad after all."

She blushed. "Of course, we don't just read."

REFLECTION: What do you stand to gain by letting go of television at dinner? What might you gain by being the first to reach out?

HABIT 9

Thanks for the Memories

PROMPT: When you're getting ready for bed

HABIT: Mentally review your day and then thank your beloved for some action, word, or experience. If you're getting ready together, tell her or him in that moment. If you're the first to bed, tell your partner before you retire, along with a goodnight kiss. If you're the last to bed, write it down for your spouse to find in the morning.

PURPOSE: We all have a negativity bias. This means that we naturally tend to notice what's going wrong in our world. This was selectively advantageous for much of human history. Our ability to scan for problems allowed us to avoid mortal danger—say, saber-toothed tigers lurking outside our cave—and thus pass on our genes. Our anxious ancestors avoided the tigers, whereas the blissed-out navel-gazers became lunch, thus leaving no descendants!

We may be wired to survive but that doesn't mean we're wired to be happy. While developing a habit of appreciation might not have kept you alive on the plains of prehistoric Africa, today it will make you more happily coupled.

Habitually demonstrating gratitude for your mate's recent behavior does several things. First, your partner feels appreciated. And when your partner feels appreciated, he or she opens up to love and warmth. Second, as you focus on what in your world is going well, you begin to see more and more circumstances, actions, and sweet moments for which to be grateful.

Dealing with life's challenges is largely a matter of where you direct your attention. When you shine a flashlight on problems, often you will see more problems. But when you shine the flashlight on all the things you appreciate about your partner, you increase your own satisfaction with the relationship. Gratitude is habit forming.

NOTE: It is not necessary for this to be a tit-for-tat habit. Be willing to offer an appreciation with no expectations for reciprocation. View it as a gift given freely, regardless of the response.

Although working with Daniel has many benefits, it's very easy for our work life to spill into our home life. One night as we were getting ready for bed, we began to discuss work. As I was putting on my nightgown, we created a to-do list that involved client billing, social media posting, and article writing.

While brushing my teeth, my mind was like a runaway train. I knew from experience that with my mind chugging along at full steam, I would have trouble falling asleep. As I worried about insomnia, my brain got even more addled; I imagined being too tired the next day to complete the to-do list we'd just constructed.

Dan watched me taking off my makeup, noting that I was sighing in that way that indicated I was superstressed. He came over, put his hand on my shoulder and said, "Did I tell you today how fabulous your article was? I know it will help a lot of people."

"Oh, really?" I began to breathe a little deeper.

"And," he continued, "did I mention how much I appreciate that you took care of the laundry today?"

"Ahhh," I exhaled, and felt my shoulders relax. My breathing got slower and smoother. His simple exclamations of gratitude made me feel more relaxed . . . more appreciated. That night, I slept like a baby.

Now, when Dan is pulling out the dental floss, I offer a daily memory with a word of thanks for him. He usually follows suit, and we engage in a Ping-Pong game of gratitude.

I can attest that when you develop this habit, the energy of going to bed together will be charged with a cascade of appreciation.

Warning: Doing this exercise may not lead to immediate slumber (wink).

REFLECTION: How does a daily gratitude practice improve your own overall satisfaction in the relationship?

HABIT 10

Shake It Up, Baby

PROMPT: Before you go into your bedroom at night

HABIT: Stand outside the bedroom door and shake off the stresses of the day. Relax your shoulders, and then shake your right leg, your left leg, your right arm, and your left arm. Use your right hand to "sweep" energy off the front of your body (from head to toe). Then use your left hand to "sweep" energy off the back of your body. Spend a moment bouncing on the balls of your feet as you continue to shake your body and exhale deeply. Let the day's mind-clutter shake off.

PURPOSE: Shaking is a simple and effective stress management tool. Shaking your body relaxes your muscles, lubricates joints, increases circulation, gives your mind a break, releases energy blocks, and discharges excess energy. In Qi Gong, a form of Chinese energy medicine, "shaking the tree" (i.e., body) is considered an important exercise to relieve stress and prepare the body for relaxation.

When you consciously release stress before you enter the sanctuary of the bedroom, you clear out mental and physical clutter so you can transition peacefully to your resting spot. There, you will be free and clear, either to be with your mate, read together, chat, have sex, cuddle, or simply fall asleep without the usual racing mind.

I often talk with couples about good sleep hygiene. I typically recommend that couples do not discuss loaded topics late at night. I ask them to refrain from watching the news after 9 P.M. or bringing work to bed. I also recommend the ultimate happiness habit: going to bed at the same time.

Although this seems a simple activity that many couples take for granted, for other couples, it feels like a Herculean task. Barbara and Bill were reluctant, at first, to try to change their bedtime pattern. Barbara was a night owl and enjoyed her quiet time after Bill went to bed. Bill was sad that he always fell asleep alone, but he understood that they had different internal clocks and work schedules.

In the end, they agreed to go to bed together at least two nights per week. If necessary, Barbara would go to bed with Bill and then sneak out again after he fell asleep so she could stay up with her favorite magazines.

After a few weeks of this, Barbara reported that even though it was nice to cuddle with Bob and have that connection, she felt agitated as she waited for him to sleep so she could get up. In fact, she went into the bedroom feeling anxious and stressed.

However, after engaging in the "Shake It Up, Baby" habit each night before she entered the sanctuary of the bedroom, she experienced an unexpected shift. Barbara told me, "I felt so relaxed after shaking for three or four minutes that I actually fell asleep before Bob! I guess I'll have to find another time to read my magazines!"

REFLECTION: Are you vigilant about protecting the sacred space of the bedroom, or do you let other things take priority?

HABIT 11

Life and Breath

PROMPT: Before you fall asleep

HABIT: Lay your finger across your partner's upper lip, like a finger mustache. Feel his/her breath gently on your finger. Silently (or aloud) give thanks that your beloved is alive and beside you.

PURPOSE: Being aware of your mortality (and that of your spouse) is useful because it means that we stop taking our time for granted. Against the backdrop of death, every moment matters. After all, one of you will outlive the other. Rather than hide from this reality, use it to heighten your awareness and appreciation.

Mystics and spiritual practitioners worldwide make a habit of looking at death head on. They might meditate with mala beads made of camel or yak bone in order to heighten reflection on impermanence. Some of the mala beads are even carved into the shape of skulls. We're not suggesting you go that far, but a habit that will be a mindful reflection on your time together will strengthen the love you feel for one another.

She sat across from me in my office with her body slumped in the chair. She seemed unable to even hold up her head. This was our first session, and her husband had died three weeks previously. Her breath was ragged as she choked back sobs and told me of the night that she found him. She had woken up in the middle of the night and found that he wasn't in bed. Wondering where he could be, she went downstairs and found him on the kitchen floor. He had recently turned forty-four years old.

Normally I can listen with compassion and not get dragged down the rabbit hole of grief. It's the only way I can do my work effectively. But in this instance, I felt almost as if a dentist had covered me in a leaden blanket. I felt weighted down . . . heavy. My head also slumped back in my chair. I felt paralyzed with her grief.

Perhaps it was because she was exactly my age, with children exactly the same age as mine. Perhaps it was because her relationship with her husband sounded very much like my relationship with Daniel, close and intimate. Whatever the reason, I felt her pain with an unusual intensity.

I listened as she implored to the heavens how she would give anything to have one more night, one more day beside her beloved. That night as I slipped into bed beside Daniel, I was keenly aware of the precious gift of life. The normal complacency that I might usually feel melted at the realization that our tomorrow together was not guaranteed. As I felt his breath on my hand, I knew that I was fully in the moment, aware of and grateful for his presence.

REFLECTION: If you were aware of death every night, how would it change the way you lived during your days?

CHAPTER 4

Let's Get Physical: Habits to Share Your Bodies

In the 1960s, scientist Harry Harlow conducted a series of controversial experiments with baby rhesus monkeys to determine the effect of affection and love on infants. The baby monkeys were separated from their biological mothers and were nourished by a "surrogate" mother: a metal dispenser that offered food and water. Not surprisingly, these poor monkeys, deprived of maternal warmth and touch, failed to thrive and, in fact, suffered severe psychological and emotional distress.

We are, quite simply, wired to be physically connected to others. Even the stereotypical gender difference in the bedroom (men want sex and women want to cuddle) indicates that both genders essentially desire physical interaction.

While we may receive touch from our friends, our parents, our children, and even from our pets, the most intimate touch of all comes through the romantic couple relationship. Within the confines of this sacred relationship, touch is intimate, arousing, playful, sexual—and essential.

Most couples find that they touch frequently when they are courting. But as time goes by, their rate of touching drops drastically. Physical affection creates a bond—everything from a stroke on the head, the holding of hands, passionate kisses, and long leisurely mornings in bed. All these and more are vital for extraordinary love.

The following habits will make it easy to sprinkle your days with touch. Do so and watch your love bloom.

HABIT 12

Necking

PROMPT: When you are in a car together at a red light

HABIT: Gently touch the back of the neck of your beloved.

PURPOSE: From the moment we're born, we crave human touch. It's as vital as the air we breathe. The health benefits of regular touch include lower stress levels, less anxiety and depression, an enhanced immune system, and even increased pain tolerance.

As a form of communication between lovers, it's a tangible expression of care, involvement, and support. The back of the neck, in particular, is a powerhouse of nerve endings. Touch in this way creates a powerful energetic bond. To do it regularly, as part of your daily routine, keeps that connection alive and well.

Forty people, participating in a group meditation, sat with their eyes closed in complete and total silence. Most were cross-legged, sitting on the floor in the lotus position. Several, including myself, were sitting upright in a chair. I felt wrapped in the comforting and densely calm energy that emerges when several dozen people join their minds in a common goal.

And then, spontaneously, I reached out to touch Daniel who was sitting on the floor directly in front of me. As I wrapped my palm around the back of his neck, he breathed in slowly and deeply. At that moment, I felt a tangible, palpable connection . . . almost as if an electric current had been generated between us. In the midst of this room of focused concentration, our sense of oneness was heightened by a simple touch.

Fast forward several years later . . . Daniel and I decided to take our five children on a once-in-a-lifetime trip to Europe. Part of the celebration was to honor our oldest daughter's recent graduation from high school with the recognition that we were moving into a new chapter of our life as a family.

We rented a large van and headed off on our tour. Although any group of seven people may experience stressful moments in a car together, the dynamics of a blended family can be especially challenging. I was concerned that Dan and I would lose our connection to each other. In fact, I was quite anxious that the car rides, in particular, would be nothing short of chaos.

During a daylong outing, early on in the trip, I remembered that magical connection we experienced during the meditation. And so, in a giant minivan on a highway, I reached over and gently touched his neck. Ahhh, yes!

For the rest of the three-week trip, whether kids were sleeping in the back, chattering about our itinerary, playing car games, arguing, or singing, every now and then I would reach over and wrap my hand on the back of my beloved's neck. Sigh. Relief. Connection. You could say that we were "necking" our way through the entire vacation.

REFLECTION: Is sharing affection through touch easy for you or difficult? How did you experience touch when you were a child?

Strawberry

PROMPT: During dinner preparations—or right before you sit down to dinner

HABIT: Stop whatever it is you are doing, go up to your beloved, and then give him or her a big, show-stopping, romantic Hollywood-style kiss.

PURPOSE: Kissing on the lips is a shockingly intimate act. You might kiss other people on the cheek or forehead, but kissing deeply on the lips is reserved for your partner. Giving him a romantic, intentional kiss—not a rote peck on the lips—confirms to your companion that he is "the one."

New couples usually kiss frequently whereas longer-term couples tend to drop this gesture. In many cases kissing becomes only a prelude for sex. In fact, some people avoid intimate kissing for fear that it will lead to sex.

What you need to do is get into the habit of kissing for its own sake. Stop what you're doing and, even in the midst of chaos, make this loving connection.

In a classic Buddhist story a woman is chased by tigers. She eventually comes to the edge of a cliff, notices a vine growing over the cliff, and climbs down it in hopes of escape. But as she looks below, she sees that there are tigers on the ground as well.

In the midst of this dilemma, she notices a small mouse nibbling on the vine above her. Tigers above, tigers below, and a failing rope. At first she panics. But then she notices, clinging to the cliff, a single ripe strawberry. She plucks the fruit, pops it in her mouth, and savors it thoroughly.

What could this all mean? Her life is about to end and she's savoring a strawberry? Well, yes, that's exactly the point. The tigers are meant to represent birth and death. By living, each of us is caught between these two realities. The mouse represents life as inconvenient, difficult, and dangerous. But the choice to savor and enjoy our blessings while we can—even in the midst of mortality and challenges—is to really live.

One night, while dinner was waiting to be assembled, while cats were circling for their food, while children were asking for help with homework, while the dishwasher needed to be emptied, while the table needed to be set, while the mail was stacked on the counter—in the middle of the mayhem, I saw my strawberry. I walked up to Dan and gave him a big, slow smooch.

A collective, "Ewwwww! Gross!" arose from the children. But I'm happy for them to see intimacy being modeled. Maybe one day, many years from now, they'll offer their beloved a beautiful kiss, right in the midst of their own dinner preparations.

REFLECTION: What gets in your way of offering your mate the gift of a kiss?

HABIT 14

Some Body

PROMPT: When you get out of the shower or bath and are drying off with a towel

HABIT: With the reverence that you would use toward a newborn baby, dry off your body parts with tenderness and thank them for their amazing functionality. Thank each specific body part for allowing you to move through your life.

PURPOSE: When you build the habit of recognizing your body for the miraculous creation that it is, you cultivate a loving tenderness toward it. And, as you do that, you offer your partner a chance to participate in this tenderness and extend the same feelings toward his body.

When you become more comfortable with your body, you become more confident. There is nothing sexier than a person who is totally at home in her or his own skin. You'll be able to get naked more easily and will have more enthusiasm for sharing your body with your beloved with an unreserved passion.

For more than two decades in my office, I have heard women and men of all ages, all shapes, and all sizes tell me they are not comfortable in their own bodies. Unfortunately, this insecurity often affects their marriages.

Thirty-year-old Margaret came from a long line of overweight individuals and had always been self-conscious about her body. She told me that she had never actually been naked with her husband of five years. Instead she always wore a nightgown when they made love. She was filled with shame.

Margaret confessed, "Harry is always telling me that I'm beautiful and it really hurts him that I won't get naked in front of him. But if he sees this roll of flab, he's going to be disgusted by me."

Although Margaret had joined weight-loss programs in the past, she had never made much progress. I suggested to her that that she needed to love her body now, exactly as it was. Then, she would be in a better position to continue loving her body as she lost weight. If she didn't lose weight, she would still love her body.

"How is that possible," she sighed. "How could I love a leg like this?"

"Are you glad that you can walk with that leg?" I asked. "Do you know what someone in a wheelchair might give for a leg like that? Doesn't Harry love that leg?"

As I worked with Margaret over the next six months, she used this habit every day to develop a more loving relationship with her body. One day, she came out of the shower and was telling her foot that she loved it when Harry walked in. She grabbed a robe to cover herself.

"What in the world are you doing?" he asked.

She told him that she was learning to love her body so she could be naked in front of him.

When he heard this, he was so moved that he embraced her and told her that he loved every part of her body just as it was.

It wasn't long before Margaret moved from a nightgown to a T-shirt to naked with the lights off and, finally, even naked during the day.

She now had a more appreciative relationship with her body, and the end result was that her marriage was happier. Harry was delighted with the change in her behavior. "He really does love me," she said. "All of me, no matter what I look like, no matter what I weigh."

REFLECTION: How would you make love differently if you completely accepted and loved your body?

HABIT 15

Teddy Bear

PROMPT: During foreplay

HABIT: As you see and touch your partner, say, "I love your body today, tomorrow, and throughout time" or other sweet, loving words that demonstrate your eternal connectedness.

PURPOSE: Developing the habit of letting your spouse know that you accept and love his or her body in spite of its changes helps your mate feel continually cherished. It's perfectly natural to want to feel attracted and attractive to your spouse. But your bodies are always changing, and you need to constantly introduce yourself to your spouse's body.

Since it might be natural for your mate to feel self-conscious about physical changes, or even embarrassed, through this habit you consistently convey the message that you love her or him unconditionally.

As you encourage your mate to feel comfortable in his or her own changing skin, your sex life will improve and your level of intimacy and connectedness will grow.

She was in her mid-thirties, a stunningly beautiful woman. She sat across from me with perfect hair, perfect nails, and a perfectly accessorized outfit. With tears in her eyes, she told me that she hated her body because she couldn't get into her size 2 jeans anymore.

Lovely Laura had spent thirteen years of her life as a professional model, steeped in an industry that prizes youth and beauty. For more than a decade, her self-worth had been measured by her ability to look slender and stunning. For the past five years, however, she had turned her attention to getting married and having a beautiful baby girl. Her size 2 jeans were a thing of the past.

"I have to find a way to lose weight," she stuttered tearfully. "I can't even get naked in front of my husband anymore. I'm sure he finds me disgusting. He married a size 2."

"And he married a woman in her twenties, but now you're in your thirties," I replied. "Your body has changed and will keep changing. Forty will look different than today, and fifty will look even more different. *His* body is changing too, you know."

She didn't look soothed. I changed tactics and asked, "Did you ever have a teddy bear or stuffed animal that you really loved when you were growing up?" Surprised, she thought about that and answered, "Of course—I had Mr. Tippy." Upon examination, I learned that she still had Mr. Tippy at the top of her closet, though now he was worn down and missing an eye.

"And do you still love him? Is he beautiful to you?" I asked.

She grinned, "It's the story of the Velveteen Rabbit, right?"

"Exactly," I confirmed. *The Velveteen Rabbit*, written by Margery Williams in 1922, was the story of a worn stuffed rabbit who is so beloved and worn out over time that in the end he becomes "real."

Even with good habits for healthy aging, your body will still change over time. Wishing it would stay the same is a fantasy. Get into this habit and become "real" with your spouse. It is much more deeply satisfying than falseness, embarrassment, or fear.

REFLECTION: Is it as easy to accept the changes in your own body as it is to accept your spouse's?

HABIT 16

I Witness

PROMPT: If you find yourself in a heated discussion (a.k.a., conflict) and you're getting triggered, activated, and/or acting in a bad way (such as cursing, name calling, blaming, criticizing, or acting irrationally)

HABIT: Turn your attention to your body and report on what you're experiencing. Say out loud, "I notice in my body that . . . my heart is racing (or my throat is tight, or my voice is getting shrill)." Be a witness to your bodily sensations and share them with your partner. Then start to lengthen and deepen your breath. Watch your body changing. Say the words, "Breathing in, I am calm. Breathing out, I relax."

PURPOSE: Interrupting an argument to focus on your inner body's response is a powerful technique for self-regulation. During a heated discussion your amygdala (the alarm bell of your nervous system) is activated. By focusing on breathing deeply, you activate the parasympathetic nervous system, which calms the alarm response.

By labeling your body responses, you shift your attention from the emotional to the physical. As your partner witnesses you doing this, the steps of your usual dance are redirected. When you consistently use this response to an argument, you will gradually rewire your brain to be less reactive, less angry, and more peaceful.

George and Sally were discussing a point of contention in my office. They were planning to visit Sally's relatives in upstate New York. Even though George had agreed to go, he wasn't exactly looking forward to the trip—Sally was taking this personally.

"I don't understand why you don't *want* to go. I always happily go to visit your folks, which is a lot more out of the way," Sally pressed.

George rolled his eyes. "I've already told you . . . I don't like the drive, and I don't like how your dad always drinks too much and then corners me to discuss politics. I said I would go, though, so why do you have to make a federal case about this? You can't make me *enjoy* it."

Sally got tearful and said in a loud voice, "I just want a little support—is that too much to ask?" She stood up hastily. "You know what? I'm outta here. I can't discuss this with you. You're never on my side." She took a step toward the door.

"Wait," I said. "Sally, I know you're feeling frustrated but I'd like you to wait a minute. This is important. Can you just say out loud what's happening in your body?"

"Huh?" she responded.

"Start by noticing your heart rate . . . and where the tension is in your body . . . just say out loud what you notice in your body."

Sally slowly told us that her heart was racing a million miles an hour. She felt as if she had been kicked in the gut. Her throat was on fire, and she knew she was talking loudly.

"Excellent," I encouraged her. "Now, if you'll just sit down, let's try some deep breathing to get your heart rate down." Sally, George, and I all inhaled to the words, "Breathing in, I am calm" and exhaled to the words, "Breathing out, I relax."

After Sally cooled down, she was able to talk from the heart, without defensiveness. She explained to George that she felt hurt and wanted to feel his support. George too was able to hear her vulnerability. He told her that his showing up was his way of loving and supporting her.

A session that could have ended in disaster instead culminated with a hug, thanks to a little body-based awareness.

REFLECTION: What might you discover if you remained calm during one of your same old arguments?

HABIT 17

Tune Up

PROMPT: When one of you is exhausted at the end of a long day—or feels ill—and simply doesn't have the energy to talk

HABIT: The more energetic of you puts his or her hands on the head of the exhausted one. Put one hand behind your partner's skull and one hand on the forehead, essentially cradling his or her head between your hands. Breathe deeply as you hold the head for up to several minutes. Let an energy current flow from your hands to your partner. You can do this while she or he is lying down or sitting. (If you want your partner to do this to you, you could ask for a "tune up.")

PURPOSE: Attunement is a form of relaxation, similar to reiki, in which the body's electrical energy is shared through the giver's hands. With attunement, you achieve a feeling of balance through moving this energy in the body's endocrine system. Your body is an integrated electrical system. When you are touched by another, you can literally feel the connection.

The head is also the home of three primary glands (pineal, hypothalamus, and pituitary) and thus is an ideal area for receiving electrical energy. The relaxing, soothing, nonverbal comfort of this position is perfect for the partner who is simply too tired, or ill, to speak.

Marley loved her job as a high school English teacher. In fact, it was a coveted job in a good school district. However, Marley's personality was naturally introverted. She was socially adept, but she needed quiet time to replenish herself.

Marley's husband, Brian, was an extrovert, refueled by social interaction. Although Marley and Brian professed to be happily married, they did have an ongoing conflict about how to spend their evenings together.

When Brian came home, he wanted to chat about his day. Marley was worn out from interacting with the twenty-five students in her classroom and the dozens of colleagues at her school. She wanted to connect with Brian, but she didn't want to talk.

I worked to instill the "Tune Up" habit in Brian as a way of helping Marley feel replenished and to shift her depleted energy. Doing this exercise once would feel nice, I explained, but doing this together daily would create a shift in their interactional pattern.

Marley was touched that Brian spent up to five minutes at night holding her head between his palms and allowing her the silence that she craved. It allowed the evening to progress between them with more understanding and compassion.

REFLECTION: How might the energy shift between you if you were willing to offer this gift of nonverbal attunement?

HABIT 18

Birthday Suit

PROMPT: When you're not feeling the old passion but wish you were

HABIT: Imagine your spouse . . . naked. Let yourself take in the visual, tactile, and aromatic details. Don't focus on only the sexual details, but also appreciate the unique and attractive characteristics of your spouse's body. Imagine the special details that only you could know.

PURPOSE: This visualization habit will stimulate both your emotional and physical attraction to your spouse. How often do you intentionally imagine your spouse naked?

Visualization techniques involve focusing your mind on images and allowing yourself to believe that they are real. Since your body cannot tell the difference between an image in your head and the real thing, visualization can change your emotional and physical reactions to external stimuli.

When you visualize the attractive aspects of your spouse's naked body, you can shift out of negative or resistant feelings that might have developed.

Have you ever been to a nude beach?

Daniel and I went to a nude beach in southern Spain, and I have to say that the experience was extremely eye-opening. Naked bodies were here, there, and everywhere: young and old, thin and fat, sitting and standing—naked bodies moving in all directions enjoying the sun and the sand.

My first response to all this nudity was to avert my eyes in embarrassment. My second response was to stare. But after a while I began to develop a simple appreciation for the beauty of the human body. Especially sweet was noting Dan's body amid other naked people, knowing that usually I am the only one to see him in his birthday suit.

The most striking result of this experience is that I can now easily summon an image of Dan's body with all its details against turquoise waters and white sand. Visualization of your spouse's body can reinvigorate feelings of connection, playfulness, youth, intimacy, and sensual desire. Bring to mind both the sexy and ordinary details of your dear one's physical form.

REFLECTION: What might happen if you awaken your sexuality?

I Wanna Hold Your Hand

PROMPT: When you're walking with your spouse in public

HABIT: Hold hands!

PURPOSE: This habit may seem like Relationship 101 advice because of its simplicity. However, most couples stop holding hands after their courtship phase. Holding hands is an easy habit to get into and a good way to keep touch in your marriage.

Charles and Elizabeth Schmitz, coauthors of *Building a Love That Lasts: The Seven Surprising Secrets of Successful Marriage*, have been conducting research on successful couples for almost three decades. They have interviewed thousands of happy couples on six continents, and their findings are remarkably consistent. One of their findings is that happy couples touch each other frequently. In fact, they touch each other whenever they can. The message is, "I love you so much that I simply can't help but touch you."

While it's healthy to hold hands in private, when you hold hands in public you communicate a message of mutual commitment. You share a sign to yourselves and to the world that you are spoken for and that you protect this relationship.

Some people protest that it doesn't feel natural to hold hands or that they didn't grow up in a touchy-feely family or culture. Although this feeling is understandable, it's important to let go of your reservations. Your brain is wired to touch in ways that relieve stress and communicate safety and attachment. Even if it feels awkward at first, reach out and hold your spouse's hand.

Julianne had tears in her eyes. "Last weekend we went out Christmas shopping and my husband never once walked beside me," she said.

"Was it too crowded on the streets?" I asked.

"No, he says that it's because he has long legs and I have short legs and so I can't keep up with him. He's always about four steps ahead of me, and I hate it." She reached for my tissue box beside the couch.

Julianne came alone to sessions but frequently lamented her husband's behavior. She was hopeful that even if he didn't come to counseling with her, she could learn some ideas that she could bring to Eric and improve their relationship.

I suggested that the next time they went out together, she reach for his hand and explain that she really wants to hold his hand. "Let him know how important it is to you—and to the relationship," I said.

The next month Julianne reported that things were going well with the handholding "project." She confided, "At first I had to practically jog to keep up with him, but now he has slowed his pace. Last weekend, he actually reached for *my* hand." Success.

REFLECTION: Do you want the world to know that you are attached to your mate?

HABIT 20

Footsie

PROMPT: During a commercial when you're watching television

HABIT: Put your foot playfully on that of your partner. Stroke her foot with yours. Make eye contact for a moment to confirm the connection and add a wink or grin. If you're close enough, you may also want to rub her foot with your fingers and/or gently massage her feet.

PURPOSE: When you're watching television together at the end of a day, usually you are tired and need to relax. It is not a time to bring up intense conversations or scheduling details. But just as you can use the entertainment as a means to unwind, you can use the commercials as a time for nonverbal connection.

Footsie is a playful, flirtatious behavior that engenders a sense of secretive intimacy. Use this habit to spark a loving connection while you're zoning out.

Jasmine was complaining to me about her husband, Spencer. "He either ignores me completely or falls asleep when I try to talk to him at night."

"He falls asleep in the middle of your conversation?" I asked, confused.

"Well, you know," she replied, "He usually is lying down on the couch next to me at night and I'm talking to him, and the next thing you know, I hear him snoring."

I asked, "What time of night are you talking about?"

She sniffed, "Usually nine at night, maybe ten."

"Well no wonder," I told her. "You should never try to have conversations that late at night if your husband is tired. In fact, once he hits the couch, you need to know that his brain is offline."

"But I feel so lonely when we're both in our separate worlds," she complained. "What can we do to feel close then if he won't even talk to me?"

"Is there anything you used to do when you were dating that you enjoyed? Something that made you feel close, something simple and nonsexual, but without words?" I coaxed.

She thought about that for a minute—and then popped out a solution, "We used to play footsie. Mostly in restaurants. I would slip my foot up his leg and no one knew. We used to get such a kick out of that."

"Perfect," I said. "Try it during the commercials."

The next week Jasmine reported that the simple, playful touch helped her feel better as they watched television together. "And some nights, he didn't even fall asleep on the couch," she said, grinning.

REFLECTION: If television were a time of connection rather than isolation, would you feel differently about it as a nighttime activity?

HABIT 21

Coast to Coast

PROMPT: When you see your lover sitting in front of a computer (regardless of whether she or he is involved in business or leisure pursuits)

HABIT: Walk past your spouse from behind and gently sweep your hand from one shoulder, across her back, to the other shoulder.

PURPOSE: Touch is a powerful way to communicate to your husband or wife that you cherish him or her. When you use this habit mindfully, you intentionally connect with your dear one.

Sitting by yourself at a computer is an isolating activity that has the potential to drive the two of you apart and make you feel disconnected. However, when you develop the habit of touching your mate when she's at the computer, you reassure her of your presence and your connection.

Veronica and Bradley had an intimate marriage. When they first came to see me, I was impressed with how close they sat to each other on the couch, how they held hands, and how they spoke positively about each other.

So why had they come for counseling? Because Bradley's adult daughter, Cindy, had died of cancer. Bradley was completely devastated by the loss and found himself withdrawing behind a wall of silence. Veronica and Bradley had only been married for five years, a second marriage for both of them.

Veronica hadn't known Cindy very well, though she, of course, was saddened by the tragic death.

"I don't know how to help Bradley," Veronica lamented. "If I bring it up, he changes the topic. He knows I will support his sadness, but he won't share it with me."

"People grieve in different ways," I responded. I looked at Bradley and asked, "What would you like from Veronica?"

He answered slowly, "I just want to know she's there ... that's all ... I really don't want to talk about my grief. I'm not a verbal person and she knows that."

They worked together from home, spending hours each day in front of their computers. I suggested that Veronica try this shoulder sweep habit whenever she walked behind Bradley, just to let him know that she was there.

Months later I got an e-mail from Veronica. She told me how helpful it was for her to learn that her physical presence was comforting to Bradley. She'd gotten into the "Coast to Coast" habit, used it freely, and both of them loved it.

REFLECTION: How many times do you pass your spouse in your house without connecting?

PART III

Communication-Building Habits

Was there a time when you felt you could tell your partner anything? He was so easy to talk to then . . . she really listened to you and was curious.

Generally most couples can remember a time when they felt they could communicate effortlessly with each other. It was part of the chemistry that created the initial bond. But all too easily the sense of mutual discovery can give way to communicating about bills, kids, work, projects around the house, and extended-family commitments.

When a couple tells me that they cannot communicate, usually what they mean is that they argue frequently, can't be honest with each other, don't feel heard, and/or don't feel valued in the relationship. In other words, simple interactions begin to lack warmth, courtesy, and kindness. When this unhealthy dynamic continues, virtually every conversation becomes unsatisfying and so, not surprisingly, couples begin to spend less time together.

However, it is possible to learn the skills to hear and be heard once again. Further, it's possible to ingrain these skills through adopting habits of communication. Having laid the groundwork of connection, along with brushing up on a few skills, it is possible to work together as a couple.

This section of the book will help you build a pattern of more effective communication, both when you're spending time alone together on a date (Chapter 5) and even when you're in the midst of a conflict (Chapter 6).

Shall We Dance? Habits on a Date with Your Mate

I sat on the floor in a room with approximately nine other women. Each of us had a small blanket in front of us on which was positioned a beautiful, healthy infant. This was my first of many "Mommy and Me" classes.

The discussion leader opened by saying, "I want to talk about your marriages." The women in the circle made a collective groan.

She continued, "I know you may not be thinking about this but that little bundle of joy in front of you has one job only: to grow up and leave you in the dust. So keep your relationship with your husband vibrant. He's the one who will still be around in eighteen years. *Go out on dates!*"

What she might have specified was, "Go out on *good* dates." Time alone together doesn't automatically result in reconnection and romance. In fact, a bad date (like bad sex) can leave you feeling lonelier than ever. You don't want to be the couple fighting over loaded topics, interacting as if you're at a business meeting, or sitting over dinner in awkward silence.

The following date habits will help you reach the goal of special, undivided time together . . . time that will enhance the "us" space and recharge your relationship.

HABIT 22

The Dating Game

PROMPT: Just before you go on a date—either a date in your own living room or a date out on the town

HABIT: Find a quiet place, maybe sitting on your bed. Close your eyes and spend a few moments bringing back the feelings of your courtship. Try to imagine a specific place and time of day when you were together. What did your body feel like at that moment? Do you remember your thoughts? Summon the sense of excitement, confusion, and anticipation of those early days. Each time you use this habit, either revisit the same memory or think of different occasions.

PURPOSE: Falling in love is likely one of life's greatest joys. The pleasure centers of the brain are constantly awash with feel-good chemicals such as dopamine and norepinephrine.

Reminding yourself of that exciting time, using a detailed visualization to summon the feeling in your body, helps engage you in your relationship and promote anticipation before your date.

When you spend time reviving heady feelings from the past, you infuse the present with old-fashioned romance. When you siphon a bit of that falling-in-love energy and inject it into your consciousness before a date, you fan the flames of desire.

Samantha told me that she and Roger never had a chance to go out on dates. They had two young children and a big problem with babysitters. Either no one was available or Samantha and Roger didn't feel that they could spare the money for a sitter on top of the expense of dinner.

I suggested that they put the kids down by 8 P.M. and then have a private dinner by the fireplace in their home . . . just the two of them. I instructed

Samantha to treat it like a "real date." For her, this meant changing out of her sweatpants and putting on jewelry.

"As you're getting ready," I told her, "I want you to spend a few minutes with your eyes closed imagining a time when you and Roger were first dating and falling in love." She agreed.

At our next session, Samantha was eager to report back on the big date. She said that it had been a huge success. "It really helped to start the date with that visualization," she said. "I pictured our first kiss, which happened to be on the Fourth of July." She continued with a gentle laugh, "There really were fireworks! I haven't thought of that kiss in years—maybe a decade!"

I smiled, "That's wonderful! How did the memory impact the date?"

"I was more relaxed when we started and absolutely determined that we needed our time together. I was clear with the girls that they had to stay in bed and read until they fell asleep."

Samantha added, "I guess reminiscing also put me in the mood because I found that I just wanted to kiss Roger for most of the date!" She blushed as she continued, "He said we should have a date every week."

REFLECTION: How would a date with your mate be different if you started it with the eyes of someone falling in love?

HABIT 23

Better to Give

PROMPT: As you officially "begin" your date

HABIT: Give your beloved a compliment. You could compliment his appearance or tell him something you appreciate or admire about him. Try saying, "One thing I deeply love about you is . . ." or "You look terrific in that shirt," or "I'm so lucky to be going out with *you*." If you happen to be on the receiving end of a compliment (which is sometimes harder than giving the compliment), rather than negate it or deflect it, give the gift of gracious acceptance (smile and say, "Thank you").

PURPOSE: Generating positive energy with a compliment is a sound investment in your relationship. Dr. John Gottman, a leading researcher about relationship stability and author of many books, including *The Seven Principles for Making Marriage Work*, studied the ratio of positive to negative comments in couples. Happy and stable couples have a 20:1 ratio (20 positive interactions to 1 negative interaction). These same couples, even when having a disagreement, still maintained a 5:1 ratio. Those who sustained a less positive ratio were more likely to divorce.

The bottom line is that couples who are *saturated* with positive energy are happier. Compliments are a form of appreciation. They let your partner know that you care, that you notice him, that you pay attention to him, and that you cherish him. You can't have too much positive energy in a happy marriage, so give it freely and the investment will come back to you tenfold.

Daniel and I once took an online relationship course designed to enhance connection and passion. Part of the program was a monthly calendar with daily directives. Each day you were supposed to "give" something to your partner: the gift of listening, the gift of a compliment, a wrapped gift hidden for them to find, the gift of a poem, the gift of a household chore done without being asked, etc.

Unfortunately, I found myself more preoccupied with what Daniel was supposed to be giving me than with what I was supposed to be giving him. In the evening, I would check in with Daniel, inquiring whether he had done his exercise. After several days of this, he gently chastised me. "I think you're missing the point," he said. "You're supposed to focus on your *own* exercises, on giving to me . . . not worrying about whether you've gotten anything yet."

H'm. Oh, yeah. Ouch. He was right, of course. I had been so preoccupied with what I was going to get that I was only cursorily paying attention to what I was supposed to give.

After that, I shifted my attention to wholehearted giving. I wanted to make sure that Daniel felt valued and appreciated. I let go of my own perspective and focused on him. As it turns out, I found that I felt happier and more at peace this way. Perhaps it really *is* better to give than to receive.

REFLECTION: If you stop thinking about what you can "get" and start focusing on what you can "give," how might the dynamic between you and your partner shift?

HABIT 24

Song Birds

PROMPT: When you've embarked on your date

HABIT: Listen to music together. Bring along a favorite CD or playlist and sing or whistle along.

PURPOSE: Music has an amazing ability to lift your mood, stimulate nostalgia, and heighten emotion. Let music set the tone for your date. Perhaps you want to listen to tunes from when you first dated . . . or songs you heard together from a particular decade. Possibly you both favor a singer/composer.

Music has the power to bond you together and mingle your energies. Use it to consciously lift your spirits as you begin your celebration of spending time alone together.

Dan and I walked along the wide Hilton Head beach on a December morning, searching for shells and watching sandpipers skitter in the surf.

"*I really can't stay*," I crooned.

"*But baby, it's cold outside*," he countered.

"*I've got to go away*,"

"*But baby, it's cold outside . . .*"

Passersby looked our way as we continued our musical call and response. We were trying to memorize the lyrics to the 1944 pop standard by Frank Loesser, a tune originally intended to be a cold weather classic but that has more recently become part of the Christmas repertoire.

We had volunteered to sing in the Friday night talent show, a playful feature of the behavioral health conference where I had been presenting a workshop. Dan and I had performed in musical theater together, but we'd never sung a duet.

Suddenly we found ourselves singing on the beach, in the elevator, in the bathroom, and of course, in the shower. We had a blast with this particular song.

On the night of the big event, we were both nervous. The show was hosted by the popular self-help author, Joan Borysenko (*Minding the Body, Mending the Mind*). As each performer got up to share their act, Joan asked them, "What's your favorite color?" However, when Dan and I took the stage, Joan simply commented on how tall Dan was (he is 6' 5" and generally gets that response from people).

Then, to my surprise, Dan said to Joan, "Aren't you going to ask me what my favorite color is?" Somewhat flustered, Joan did so.

"The color of Ashley's skin," Dan replied.

"Awwwwwwwww!" It was as if we'd carried a puppy on stage. I blushed noticeably and was so surprised by this intimate comment that I could barely remember the words to our song.

Now just the first line of "Baby, It's Cold Outside" brings a smile to our lips. We picture Hilton Head, the beach, the stage, the shower (smile). Singing that song again together, we know we're in for a fun night.

REFLECTION: What song immediately brings your lover to mind? How do you feel when you sing or hum it?

HABIT 25

Through the Years

***

PROMPT: When you're waiting for your food to arrive

HABIT: Say, "I have a memory to share." Take turns sharing some happy memories from the past. Go back in time, year by year, and recall a pleasant memory in as much detail as you can. If you have trouble remembering specific years, use places you lived, places you've traveled, holidays, or kids' school years as memory touchstones. If you've been together for many years, share memories by the decade.

PURPOSE: When you systematically share happy memories with each other, you dance to the pleasant music of nostalgia. You not only fill yourselves with the spirit and emotion of wonderful times, but you may also be reminded of forgotten times or see them anew through your spouse's eyes.

Couples therapists often suggest their clients go out on a date. Of course this can mean different things for different couples—dinner out, a hike, a picnic, a coffee, a concert, a movie, a comedy club, a walk in the woods. Going out with another couple doesn't count. The purpose is to be alone together.

When I send couples out on a date, I ask them to observe the "500-yard rule." As soon as you get 500 yards from your home, you cannot discuss the following three topics:

1. Finances
2. Kids (if applicable)
3. Work

In answer to this directive, couples usually say, "What in the world are we going to talk about?"

That's when I suggest a "life review." While on their date, some couples share highlights from vacations; others go through their lives together systematically, year by year, sharing their favorite memories.

Pete and Nancy reported back to me that they hadn't gotten past 1990 because they had so much fun reviewing the '80s together. Lorraine and Arthur even remembered their hard times together, which made them aware of their strength as a couple.

One of the perks of this exercise is having the other person jog your own memory of how things unfolded. Often people will claim, "Oh, yeah—I forgot all about that experience." Also, two people will remember the same event in slightly different ways based on their own perspectives, personalities, and histories. It can bring a new understanding into your relationship to see the past through the eyes of your mate.

While living in the "now" can generate peace and calm, ironically a detour into the past can bring happiness and intimacy right into the present moment.

REFLECTION: What memory of a time with your beloved can you hold dear to your heart, a memory that will always bring a smile to your face?

HABIT 26

Gone with the Wind

PROMPT: When you are on your date and need a conversation jump-starter

HABIT: Ask your mate, "How do you think you have changed over the past year?" Then, if needed, help her recall events from the past year: new job, new home, big promotion, children growing up, an accomplishment, a disappointment, aging parents, an illness or loss. Be open and curious to whatever changes she is experiencing.

Alternately, you can use this tool to share how *you* feel you've changed in the past year: "I'd like to share with you how I think I've changed over the past year."

PURPOSE: Change is inevitable whether we like it or not. The person you fell in love with will change. She will get older, possibly wiser, and will be influenced even more by her life yet to live. Many couples find that they start to grow apart as they change. To avoid this you must face change head on.

Embracing change together by noticing it and talking about it builds intimacy. Encouraging your mate to be reflective gives her a chance to shape her experiences into words. It helps you understand her inner world. Meanwhile, sharing about your own change reveals your authentic self to your partner.

This habit builds a bridge to each other as you become aware of the changes in your midst.

My first husband used to call me "Mario" for Mario Andretti (the famous race car driver of the 1960s). I was a fearless and fast driver. However, over the next five years I developed a highway-driving anxiety. Suddenly, I was the annoying driver going *under* the speed limit.

David would say to me, "But you used to be Mario. What happened?"

"I changed . . . that's what happened," I responded. "What made you think that I wouldn't change?" (I didn't point out that he had a lot less hair on the top of his head.)

It's a funny paradox that, in a world that we know is constantly changing, we somehow think our spouses should be the exception. We are surprised if she once loved shrimp but now cannot stomach it. We are shocked that he once was thin but now is fat. And the fact that she suddenly picked up kayaking (or darts or hunting)—you didn't see that coming, did you?

I'm reminded of a wonderful couples therapist who when asked, "How can couples keep their relationship fresh and new on a daily basis?" answered, "Know that every single day, you're married to a new person." She advised that you wake up with a sense of wonder about who you're going to discover.

For better or for worse, you cannot hold still the sands of time. So rather than resist change, embrace it . . . right in the middle of a date night. Use the conversation to reflect on the past and the present, helping your mate put into words the changes he or she has been experiencing. You'll get to rediscover one another all over again.

REFLECTION: How do you resist the changes in your mate? How could you celebrate the changes in your mate?

HABIT 27

Dream On

PROMPT: While lingering over dessert and coffee

HABIT: Ask, "What do you dream will happen in the next ten years?" Spin out the trajectory of how life will be when/if this dream occurs. It could be a real possibility (such as a vacation on the horizon, when the kids are grown, when you retire) or a fantasy (if you owned a boat, if you ran a bed and breakfast, if you won the lottery). Keep asking questions and exploring the dream.

PURPOSE: When couples are first blending their lives together, they talk frequently about their hopes for the future. They fantasize about where they might live, whether to have children, what jobs they might seek, etc. And yet, after many of those dreams become reality, they stop systematically dreaming together.

As you listen to your mate, don't take anything too personally. Don't react negatively, rolling your eyes or gasping in panic. Remember, this is simply a conversation about wish and desire. See it as a way to get to know your spouse a little better.

Being curious about your spouse's inner world is an aphrodisiac. People feel attractive when someone finds them interesting.

Also, if you share your spouse's dream, you might fantasize together about how this dream might be possible. It can give you a road map as you solidify common values and goals. However, the point of the habit is to not to create a concrete plan but to have fun dreaming.

Dan and I sat across from our financial adviser. This good-natured gentleman spends his days helping people plan for the future responsibly. After an hour of jumping ten, twenty, and even thirty years into the future as we reflected on kid college years, retirement, and estate planning, I felt overwhelmed.

Russell leaned across the desk toward us conspiratorially and said, "You know, I've been in this business a long time, and things almost never turn out exactly as you imagine they will." He chuckled, "In fact, the best part seems to be dreaming about the future. The dream is usually better than the reality!"

It's true that when many people reach their long-term goals, they're a bit disappointed. Ironically, fantasizing about the future may help you enjoy the moment you're in more thoroughly.

Dreaming together is an entertaining exercise in which you write the script and play the leading roles. So spend a little time relishing the details of a dream in which all conditions are perfect, in which every problem is either solved or nonexistent. Imagine the picnic on the beach with no sunburn, the travel with no jetlag, the vacation home with no maintenance issues. Make it fun dreaming because the process itself may be the dreamiest part.

REFLECTION: Do you have a dream you've never shared with your partner?

HABIT 28

Light Bright

PROMPT: When your dear one comes back from going to the restroom

HABIT: Light up when you see your loved one. Smile, nod, stand up, lift your eyebrows, and/or pull out her chair. Intentionally touch her arm or shoulder. For added emphasis, include the words, "Wow, I'm glad you're back" or "I'm so happy to be here with you." Look at your sweetheart with adoration on your face. After all, this is the one with whom you've chosen to spend your life with.

PURPOSE: Everyone wants to feel desired. Your presence should matter to your loved one. You want to feel special, cherished, adored. Although you may be wishing that your spouse would make *you* feel this way, this tool is about making *her* feel that way. You can't control her behavior, but you can focus on and control your own.

A common complaint from unhappily coupled people is that one or the other—sometimes both—feels taken for granted. Be the light that dispels the darkness. Brighten up when you see your mate, (even without words, body language and touch can illuminate the night), doing your best to make her feel special and valued. Regardless of her reaction, you'll know that you're doing everything you can to create a climate of appreciation.

"He got me roses . . . for Valentine's Day," she stammered in the session. Trixie was a forty-eight-year-old woman coming to see me for depressive symptoms. As we untangled the strands of her life, it became evident to both of us that she was unhappy in her marriage. Her husband Ed, however, wasn't willing to come with her to see a "shrink." "That's what crazy people do," he said. Trixie, however, was just "crazy" enough to come see me.

"Was that nice for you, the roses?" I inquired.

"I don't care about stupid flowers," she said. "He gave them to me and then didn't speak to me for the rest of the night. I'd be happier if he just spent some time with me . . . I mean, if he actually *wanted* to spend some time with me . . . you know, if he'd just light up a bit when I came into the room."

Ah, lighting up like a Christmas tree at the very sight of your beloved. It's so simple but so powerful. I was reminded of a time when I came down the stairs one morning to Daniel's beaming smile (he typically wakes long before I do). I must have beamed back because he said that I was like the sun shining down on him. While I may have been his sun, it was *his* face lighting up when he saw me that filled me with warmth and light. This sense of wonder doesn't have to go away just because the honeymoon is over.

I asked Trixie if she told Ed that *she* wanted to spend time with *him*. I asked her if *she* lit up when *he* entered a room. I suggested she give these things a try. Because humans are wired to connect, we all want the same basic things: to be appreciated, to know that we matter, to be intimately connected. So, on a primal level, your mate wants the very same things that you do.

Trixie came back the next week and announced that they had gone for a walk together on the beach. "We actually had a good time," she said sheepishly. "He went in the opposite direction looking for shells, but when he came back, I 'lit up' when I saw him. He was so flustered," she said, "that he actually looked behind him to see if someone else was there." She laughed. "I told him that I was just excited to see *him* and be with him."

She blushed. "Actually, the rest of the night was better too."

REFLECTION: Do you notice any shifts in your partner's demeanor when you make an attempt to make him/her feel extra special?

HABIT 29

New Wiring

PROMPT: When you're feeling bored with the same old date routine

HABIT: Intentionally do something new: Try a new restaurant; go to a new neighborhood; try something you've never done before; taste a new food; drive a different route; eat dessert first.

PURPOSE: When you participate in a new activity together, you build fresh and stimulating experiences as a couple. This happens naturally when you're on vacation in a new place together but happens less frequently when you're on home turf. Trying new things will let you see yourself as well as your partner in a new light.

Novelty is good for keeping the brain active and for stimulating the feel-good chemical dopamine. Likewise, novelty helps keep our relationships fresh. Experimenting with something new shifts you out of old ruts that can make your relationship feel stale. If you're struggling to think of something different, check the local newspaper for ideas. Or keep an ongoing list of new things to try, which you can consult when ideas are running low.

Neuroplasticity (the brain's ability to change in response to new behaviors) research has shown that new activities cause new neural pathways to form in the brain. Therefore a simple change of routine will actually change your brain and stimulate you out of your rut. There's nothing more effective for shaking things up than trying something new!

When I suggest to couples that they try something new for a date, I'm frequently impressed with their range of creative ideas. One young couple went to a senior center to play competitive bingo. Another couple played a dinner game, going to one restaurant for appetizers, another restaurant for entrées, and still another restaurant for dessert.

So when Dan and I were planning one of our monthly dates, I came up with the idea of attending a musical mystery dinner theater. Neither of us had any idea of what to expect. What we got was a night of full-throttle audience participation. We also didn't expect the raucous, adults-only-themed humor throughout the night.

Staged in a historic inn, the production rotated the audience into five different rooms where we witnessed scenes, gathered clues, and helped enact ridiculous sketches. Our goal was to have fun while figuring out "whodunit."

Amid our rotating rooms, we laughed while women donned boas and suggestively licked popsicles. The women sang while men were given "makeovers" of green hair and bright red lipstick. Dan and I sat back, enjoying the merriment.

That is, until one of the characters corralled Dan at the front of a room, put a 40DD brassiere over his shirt, and slid grandma-size silk panties over his legs. Playing va-va-voom strip tease music, they made him parade around our group and strut his stuff. Not only did Daniel rise to the occasion, but he had us howling as he sashayed enthusiastically up and down the aisle.

"It's usually the quiet, conservative types who have the most ham in them," confided the actress who chose him. Who knew?

REFLECTION: What do you have to lose by making the extra effort to find a new kind of date night for you and your partner?

HABIT 30

Choice Cuts

PROMPT: When you get in the car after your date (or when you use any transportation to return home)

HABIT: Say to your beloved, "I choose you. I'm committed to you." Seal the deal with a juicy kiss.

PURPOSE: It's a wonderful thing to choose a life partner and make a commitment to him. Usually the wedding day or commitment ceremony is awash with the joy of your friends and family witnessing and celebrating this choice.

However, as the years go by, we often lose touch with the essence and spirit of this choice. Having made that commitment, we somehow assume that it will continue all by itself. Before you know it, we take that choice for granted and stop thinking about it. We forget that every day offers a choice to remain committed.

Letting your mate know that you still *choose* him as a spouse gives him a sense that he is important, valued, and prioritized. Sending this message on a regular basis keeps the relationship healthy and strong.

The Christmas season was upon us and I found myself standing at a long checkout line in a local bookstore. The woman in front of me turned in my direction and smiled. She said gleefully, "Glad to see that people are still buying books!"

I nodded my head in quiet affirmation, though I wasn't interested in striking up a conversation.

Undeterred, she volunteered, "I'm not even getting a holiday present. Isn't that silly? I'm getting books for me and my honey when we go on our vow renewal trip."

Okay, I bit. "Vow renewal trip?" I asked.

She told me that every year, without fail, for the past twenty-two years, she and her husband returned to Bermuda where they were married. They went back to the same beach and renewed their wedding vows.

As a couples counselor, I was impressed. As a wife, I was amazed. "You never miss a year?" I asked.

"Nope," she said. "We take our commitment very seriously." She paused. "Of course, we're getting older now, and I suppose eventually we might stop going. But the main thing is to renew our priority to each other." She thought for a moment. "Actually, we could do that anywhere . . . but then again, why not go to Bermuda while we can?"

You might not be able to take an annual trip, but you can be intentional about affirming your commitment to your honey. Even if you only briefly acknowledge that out of all the people in the universe, you choose this special one to be with, that's a powerful reminder to both of you about the sanctity of your relationship.

REFLECTION: Would you still choose this spouse if you had it to do over again?

Home Sweet Home

PROMPT: When you pull into the driveway (or walk home) after your date

HABIT: Put your hand over your heart and say, "I love our home . . . especially the _____. And I love that we live here together." Fill in the blank with something different each time you end a date, noting a beloved possession, room, or aspect of your home that you have created together.

PURPOSE: Gratitude as a regular practice is a direct route to happiness—in fact, it should become a habit. The field of positive psychology has made a study of gratitude, with the results being that grateful people have higher levels of well-being, are happier, are more satisfied with their lives and relationships, have greater resilience, and even sleep better!

Gratitude is medicine for the heart. There is a cascading effect. When you focus on gratitude, your heart opens, and you find even more for which to be grateful. The wonderful news is that gratitude is habit-forming. Like any other habit, it can be learned. So use the prompt of returning from your date as a cue to notice and feel grateful. Charge it with emotion, hold it deeply, and express it clearly.

Focus your mind on the wonderful living space that you've created together. Doing so will create a pleasant transition from the intimacy of your date into your home space.

Rachel and Roger rarely went on dates. If they did go out for dinner, they usually doubled with another couple. With three young children in the house, they almost never spent time alone together.

Their twelfth wedding anniversary was coming up and I suggested that they take the opportunity for a private date—no kids, no other couples, no extended family; just the two of them.

We went over some ground rules about what to avoid talking about (kids, work, finances) and what they might talk about (the habits in this section). They were ready for Friday night and looking forward to a special evening together.

The next week, I anticipated hearing how their big date had gone. But Rachel and Roger looked frustrated when they walked in my office. Roger blurted out, "It was all going great. We went to the restaurant that she wanted. We had some wine. We used the 'Gone with the Wind' tool and we had fun with 'Through the Years.'"

"That's terrific," I interjected. "And then . . . ?"

"Well, we were just at the entrance to the driveway," Roger continued, "and I thought for sure that we'd be making love that night. But suddenly, she started going over a to-do list . . . how I needed to go to the dump on Saturday and how I should mow the lawn and fix her bike. She even mentioned putting our taxes together. She just threw all these chores at me."

Rachel jumped in. "I'm sorry that I made him so mad but I just started thinking of all the stuff that we needed to do, and I couldn't help it. So he got all huffy and when we went in the house, he just went to his computer. That was that."

From Rachel and Roger I learned that the end of the date is almost as critical as the date itself. So as you return home from your date, fill your words with gratitude. Extend the magic as long as possible.

REFLECTION: If your date ended with a moment of intentional gratitude, how do you think it would affect the rest of the evening?

CHAPTER 6

I Second That Emotion: Habits for Couples in Conflict

From finances to parenting to sex to careers to time management to chores to—you name it, couples will fight about it. However, when it comes to a happy marriage, it's not so much *what* couples argue about that really matters. It's *how* they argue.

Based on simple interactional patterns, Dr. John Gottman, preeminent couples researcher, is able to predict with 97 percent accuracy which couples will stay together and which couples will divorce (or stay together but miserably). How does he do it? He looks for patterns created by what he calls "the Four Horsemen of the Apocalypse":

1. **Criticism** (of their personality or character)
2. **Contempt** (sarcasm/attacking)
3. **Defensiveness** (seeing self as always right and/or the victim)
4. **Stonewalling** (emotional withdrawal/the silent treatment)

When any of the Four Horsemen show up regularly in your relationship, they indicate a basic lack of respect. It doesn't really matter whether you're discussing taking out the garbage or your teenager's curfew. If you attack your spouse with contempt and criticism, or if you stonewall and act defensively, you are eroding the love between you.

However, if you habitually use antidotes to the Four Horsemen, you create a climate of collaboration. Antidotes include "I" versus "You" statements, responsibility, self-soothing, appreciation, kindness, generosity, and forgiveness. Then your challenges become a pathway for growth and deeper understanding.

The following habits will help you cut through conflict in a healthy way. With intention, you can change habituated patterns of negative responses into a new dynamic.

Half Full

PROMPT: When your beloved does that thing that he *always* does and has *always* done that totally and completely annoys you and may bring up a feeling of exasperation or contempt (this includes leaving the toilet seat up, or dropping dirty socks on the floor)

HABIT: First recognize that this is simply what your partner does and that you may not ever be able to change his behavior. Rather than experience your darling as a "half-empty glass," immediately redirect your attention to the glass half full by asking yourself, "What are three things that my honey has done for me/provided for me in the past week?" Remember that no one is perfect. Everyone (including you) is a package deal.

PURPOSE: This tool, inspired by the Japanese practice of *Naikan* (translated as "introspection"), is a structured method of self-reflection developed by Yoshimoto Ishin. It includes three questions designed to restructure your thinking and see more clearly the give and take in relationships.

The first question of the *Naikan* practice is "What have I received from this person?" The question can be asked of anyone in your life, but it is especially powerful with a romantic partner. The point is to change your focus by shifting your attention from your mate as a problem to your mate as a supporter. Gratitude then starts to overcome resentment, making the glass very full indeed.

Dan frequently cannot keep track of his cell phone . . . or his sunglasses, or his keys, or his wallet, or his hat. In fact, he temporarily "misplaces" items all the time. Now it's true that most of these things turn up sooner or later, and it's also true that Dan never frets about these losses.

However, I get frustrated by this inconvenient habit. Clearly "his" problem is really "my" problem—or rather, how I handle the situation determines whether I have a problem. Freak out: I have a problem. Accept it: I don't.

Recently I was returning from a writing retreat, and we had planned for Dan to pick me up at a certain time. However, I was done an hour earlier than expected, so I called Dan on his cell phone. No answer. H'm, that's funny. *Why isn't he answering his cell phone?* I wondered. I texted. No response.

That's when it hit me. I knew it. I just *knew* it. He had forgotten his cell phone. My gut reaction was one of super annoyance, combined with an overwhelming desire to chastise him. But of course, there was no way to reach him, and I felt powerless over the circumstances.

However, I wasn't powerless over my reaction. I wanted to feel accepting, not upset. I found a chair, took a deep breath, and settled in to change my perspective. I intentionally began to list all the things that Dan had done for me in the past week. He had generously supported me in going on this retreat, he had driven me and was planning to pick me up, he had put love notes in my suitcase . . . the list went on and on.

By the time he finally picked me up, I was calm, grateful, and thrilled to see him. I know that Dan will forget and lose his phone a hundred times more, but he never seems to lose what matters most: his love for me. For that, I can be grateful.

REFLECTION: How do you feel about your significant other when you highlight his or her wondrous qualities?

Kiss and Make Up

PROMPT: After an argument when you know that you've been critical and defensive (said unkind things, shouted, slammed something, accused, or blamed)

HABIT: After you've had a chance to calm down, go to your beloved and say, "I'm sorry. I completely missed the mark." Seal the apology with a gentle kiss.

PURPOSE: When you mess up, the best course of action is to apologize. In general, you will make mistakes in your relationship because you are an imperfect human being. Welcome to human nature! Coming to accept yourself as flawed paves the way for a humbling apology. Use the Japanese philosophy of *wabi sabi* to have compassion for yourself. *Wabi sabi* is the ability to find beauty in imperfection. Japanese artists will even build in imperfections to their artwork as a celebration of it.

Author and relationship expert Arielle Ford writes in *Wabi Sabi Love* that when you begin to embrace your own imperfections as well as your partner's imperfections, you create the foundation for true happiness.

While it takes courage to face your shortcomings, doing so will build a bridge of connection back to the other. Saying "I'm sorry" is a classic repair to a relationship rupture. It's not so much the ruptures that make or break a relationship—because damage is inevitable—it's the quality and consistency of repair that keeps a relationship healthy and happy.

I hadn't seen Delia and Jason in more than six months. We had ended our work successfully and both of them said they were happier in their marriage. They had already integrated quite a few happy habits into their daily routine and had "graduated" from our sessions with flying colors.

But here they were again sitting on my couch with matching frowns on their faces. "Tell me what's going on," I said.

Jason volunteered, "Everything was great and suddenly, ever since our vacation a month ago . . . well, things have been terrible."

"Really," I responded. "What happened a month ago?"

Delia jumped in, "Our beach vacation."

As we began to uncover what had occurred on the vacation, Delia revealed that Jason had gotten rip-roaring drunk one night, to the point that he passed out on their hotel room floor. Jason had no history of excessive drinking, but Delia had grown up with an alcoholic father, making her especially sensitive to this behavior.

After that night, Delia shut down emotionally, and neither of them had discussed the event again.

Jason looked dumbfounded as he listened to Delia's rendition of his drunken escapade. "*That's* why you've been angry for the past month? Why didn't you say something?"

Delia could only say that although she had been trying to forget the incident, she had been unable to do so.

So I asked him, "Did you ever apologize to Delia?" He sheepishly shook his head. "No, I was too embarrassed and was hoping it would blow over," he said. I suggested that it was better late than never. He turned to look at Delia and admitted that his behavior had been stupid and unacceptable. He said with emotion, "I'm so sorry that it happened and I'm so sorry that I hurt you."

Delia melted. A heartfelt apology with a kiss was all the therapy they needed.

REFLECTION: Are there things in your relationship that you need to apologize for?

HABIT 34

Let Freedom Ring

PROMPT: When you can't seem to let go of a grievance . . . when you're holding on to a grudge from the past

HABIT: Spend some time breathing. As you breathe in, say softly, "I feel better." Breathing out, say, "when I let go." As you exhale, let your body relax. Remember that *you* hold the key to your liberation from misery when you choose to let go of resentment.

PURPOSE: There is a cost to holding on to an injury: You create your ongoing distress. Clinging to a wound and blaming the other person is like holding on to a hot coal with the intention of hurling it at your adversary . . . or like ingesting poison and expecting the one you're mad at to die. Meanwhile, *you're* the one in trouble. The way to find relief is to forgive, let go, and move on. Holding on is looking backward. Letting go is moving forward.

Forgiveness is often misunderstood. It doesn't mean condoning whatever bad behavior occurred in the past. It simply means accepting that it is over and done and then deciding to cut the string of attachment to the offending memory. Forgiveness is not for the benefit of the other person. It is a choice of liberation for you and your own peace of mind.

On one of the most glorious summer days that New England had to offer, Daniel and I set off to the beach for a romantic picnic. Against the backdrop of several weeks of health challenges, financial concerns, and stress at home, we were prepared to throw our cares into the ocean and enjoy a beautiful evening together. That was the intention, at least.

As we got on the highway, I saw Dan was driving close to eighty miles an hour. "Can't you slow down?" I asked. He slowed to seventy-five. After a few minutes, I nagged again. "Why are you such a lead foot tonight? We're not even in a hurry." (Interestingly, I have heard many couples fighting over this same situation.)

Dan tried to change the subject, but I felt the need to complain yet again. "Why can't you just slow down?" And at precisely that moment, that heart-stopping image appeared behind us: a state trooper with blinking lights.

It's possible to receive a speeding ticket, shrug your shoulders, and decide not to let it ruin your evening. That was Dan's response. However, it's also possible to go berserk and spend the next hour in a tantrum. That, unfortunately, was mine.

Yes, upon reaching the beach and popping the bottle of wine, I went into a tirade that broke every "rule" of fair fighting. I am embarrassed to admit that I name called, I brought up old grievances, I catastrophized, I stonewalled (gave Dan the silent treatment), and I criticized. Basically, although I wanted to believe that Dan ruined our evening by getting a speeding ticket, I knew that I was ruining it by reacting badly.

After a while I started to walk along the beach, breathing and trying to calm myself. I thought of the many stories I have heard from clients who hold on to grievances from months, years, and decades past. I thought of the ongoing torment I have witnessed in people who are held hostage by their grudges.

But I also knew that even if I had a legitimate reason to be annoyed, the only way for me to find freedom was to look ahead rather than behind. I had to let go. And so, for the sake of my own well-being, I did.

I'm happy to report that the rest of the evening took us in a much better direction.

REFLECTION: What do you have to lose by letting go? What do you have to gain?

HABIT 35

Through Your Eyes Only

_____

PROMPT: When you're having a disagreement, especially if you are stuck on proving your position and defending yourself

HABIT: Say "Let's Switch" and then say out loud how your mate is viewing the situation. In other words, speak from his perspective as if you were seeing through his eyes (say, "I am 'Bill' and this is how I see it . . ." or "I am 'Jill' and this is my reality . . ."). Before you speak, spend a moment with your eyes closed, breathing deeply, and thinking about what life must look like through the lens of your mate's history, his personality, his experience. Once your partner adopts this habit, you can ask him to speak from your perspective.

PURPOSE: Most people, when they are having a disagreement with their spouse, only care about their own perspective. Both want to make their point, prove that they are right, and solidify their positions, but neither is empathic to the partner's point of view.

However, empathy is a powerful component of your innate emotional intelligence. When you develop the capacity to put yourself in the place of your loved one, you increase your ability to appreciate his or her position. You get to know, and therefore recognize her desires and needs. You naturally come to understand her better.

Seeing life from your partner's perspective also helps you generate the highest form of love: what the Greeks called *agape* or "selfless" love. In this form of love you sincerely care about meeting your mate's needs and not just about meeting your own.

I was listening to a meditation CD billed as a tool for increasing empathy for your partner. The man's soothing voice asked me to imagine my partner standing before me. I imagined Daniel in our backyard with me in front of him.

The voice guide asked me to gaze at my partner, looking into his eyes. "Imagine," he said, "what it must have been like for this person to be a child of five years old. Where did he live? What sorts of things did she do? . . . Now imagine your partner at the age of fifteen, a teenager. What was his life like? What challenges did she have?"

I tried my best to imagine Dan's life as a child, as a teenager. And indeed, I did feel empathy welling up in my chest. "Now think about some of the struggles that he currently faces from time to time. Think about how the past impacts him now." I felt immersed in Dan's psyche, his history, his reality.

Then, quite unexpectedly, the quiet meditative voice asked me to "jump into your partner's body and see through his eyes." Whoa. I did *not* see that directive coming. Awkwardly, I did my best to imagine what it would be like to see through the eyes of a 6' 5", 220–pound male body.

Actually, it was surprisingly easy. I could see what he might see and feel what he might feel. I gained a new understanding of some of his requests, such as his desire to go to a family party when I had other plans, or his urge to go on all-male summer camping trips.

When I "came back" into myself, I had a whole new appreciation for what it was like to be Dan navigating his world.

REFLECTION: Through your spouse's eyes, how does he or she view *you*?

HABIT 36

For Whom the Bell Tolls

———————

PROMPT: Before you begin to discuss finances

PROP: A bell, a singing bowl, or a chime.

HABIT: Sit together with a bell and ring it three times. Close your eyes and listen to the tone. Let the sound wash over and around you. Listen to each ring until the vibrations slowly dissipate into the air. After the third ring, open your eyes and say, "We're in this together."

PURPOSE: For many people, money is a loaded subject. In fact, it's the number one issue that couples argue about (followed by sex and parenting). Money brings up issues of fear versus trust, scarcity versus abundance, and insecurity versus security.

However, in an intimate relationship, what's even more important than the content is the process. In other words, it's not so important *what* you are discussing as *how* you are discussing it. Are you talking about a subject openly and thoughtfully, creating a sense of emotional safety for each other? Or are you discussing the subject with hostility and reactivity?

This habit is steeped in the tradition of mindfulness, the practice of nonjudgmental awareness. This means being focused and attentive but in a way that is accepting of whatever arises. As the bell rings and you focus on the tone, you experience presence and acceptance, without knee-jerk responses.

If you find that the discussion is getting tense, you can ask to ring the bell again as a way to settle both of you and refocus on the goal of teamwork. Also, it helps to sit next to each other as you're discussing your finances and to occasionally touch each other's hands or arms to help keep the continuity of closeness.

By reminding yourselves that you're on the same team, you attune to each other before and during a potentially challenging discussion. This climate of connection, combined with mindful attention, sets the stage for a rich conversation.

Mark and Michelle were ready for the session to begin. Their arguments about money had driven them into marriage counseling. I started the session as I always do: "Let's begin with the bell." We closed our eyes, and I went into my usual monologue, instructing them to focus on their breath and let their bodies relax. Then I said, "When you hear the sound of the bell, focus on the tone. Let the sound wash over you and take you inside to a place underneath circumstance, a place of stillness and peace. Breathe in the bell."

My clients are used to this mindfulness ritual. As we listen to the sound until it is gone, we not only relax but we become mutually present and together. The whole practice takes around sixty seconds.

Mark sighed, "I love the bell. I feel so calm when I hear that bell."

As our session progressed, the discussion of finances began to get tense. Michelle, agitated, snapped, "Mr. Save-It-for-Retirement doesn't want us to spend money on anything fun. Who knows if we'll even live until we retire. I want to live *now* and enjoy the money while we have it."

Mark rolled his eyes and said, "With that attitude, we'll be destitute in five years. It's just plain irresponsible to spend our savings."

"Okay," I interjected. "I think this is a perfect time to come back to the bell. Remember that you are in this together. Think calm. Think compromise." I rang the bell three times.

As we opened our eyes, I could tell that their energy had palpably shifted. The tension between them had drifted away on the crest of the sound waves. Michelle said softly, "Markie, honey, I know that we need to save for the future. But we need to have a little fun too. Don't you think we can find a balance?"

Mark smiled. "I'll tell you what, we're gonna buy a bell like that for us and use it every time we talk about money." We all laughed.

REFLECTION: How would your relationship improve if you could have calm discussions about your finances?

HABIT 37

Peekaboo

PROMPT: When you notice your spouse starting to blame, criticize, complain, or otherwise attack you

HABIT: Ask yourself, "I wonder what's really going on underneath?" Take a few minutes to breathe deeply and recognize that your spouse feels either unloved or unsupported and doesn't know how to get that message across effectively. Instead of reacting to the negativity, diffuse it by tenderly saying something along the lines of "I want you to know that my intention is always to love you and to support our life together."

Conversely, if you find that *you* are the one blaming, criticizing, or complaining, look within for what is really going on underneath your attack. You can lead from your vulnerability and say, "What I really need to know is that you love me and support our life together."

PURPOSE: Sue Johnson, author of *Hold Me Tight: Seven Conversations for a Lifetime of Love* and the founder of a highly effective couples therapy template (Emotionally Focused Therapy, or EFT) explains that your deepest human need is to feel securely attached in your primary relationship. When you feel a threat to this attachment, you experience an involuntary and usually unconscious panic, which often results in an unsavory protest or tantrum.

These protest behaviors of complaint, blame, and demand are a sort of primal response to emotional starvation. Unfortunately, these toxic responses tend to elicit the very thing you fear (more distance). However, as EFT teaches, when you learn to understand the deeper need beneath the behavior (both within yourself and within your partner), you're able to respond with tenderness and emotional resonance.

Marissa had a knack for getting exactly the opposite of what she really wanted from her husband Joe. She constantly complained, criticized, and blamed him. These were her common refrains:

"You always work late. You never come home in time for dinner with the family." What she really meant underneath is, "I miss you, and I feel like the children and I don't matter to you." But that's not what Joe heard. All that filled his ears was the nagging voice.

His response? He felt attacked, and he therefore shut down. He felt that he didn't even particularly want to come home early, even when he could.

"Why don't you ever help around the house? I've asked you three times already to take out the garbage. You're so lazy." Joe's response? He felt nagged and humiliated. He shut down even further. Marissa's underlying message wasn't reaching him: "I feel all alone and afraid, and I need to know that you support this life with me."

"You never want to have sex anymore. You don't even come to bed with me. It's so stupid to always fall asleep in front of the television." His response? He stayed away and pushed her still further from him. (Would *you* want to go to bed with her?) What she really meant underneath was, "I am so lonely. I need to know that you desire me as I desire you. I want to feel special to you."

How ironic that Marissa and Joe basically wanted the same thing: to feel supported, appreciated, and nurtured. However, when Marissa reacted to her sense of separation anxiety with typical "protest behaviors," she ended up creating the very thing she feared most (having Joe become even *more* distant).

In my work with Marissa and Joe, I wanted to create a safe environment in which both of them could understand their greater desire to be close to each other. I helped Marissa express her needs directly, and I helped Joe understand her needs even when she couldn't communicate them clearly.

When Joe realized that Marissa's deepest longing was to know that she was important to him, he was able to assure her of that through word and action. And when Marissa realized that Joe did support her and the family with his love, she was able to appreciate him and listen for his needs as well.

REFLECTION: What do you have to gain by hearing your spouse's true desire underneath his or her protest behaviors?

HABIT 38

Terms of Agreement

PROMPT: When you are stuck in a disagreement with your beloved

HABIT: Change the pattern of conflict by saying the words, "Yes," or "I can see that," or "I agree," or "Maybe, let's see." Above all, stop being defensive!

PURPOSE: The ego always wants to be "right." However, when you chronically disagree or insistently drive your point home, you create negative energy.

In arguments, you may notice yourself saying "But . . ." over and over. Perhaps you recognize that you're stuck behind the need to be right. However, when you diffuse the negative energy by offering agreement, you move in a new direction. It is virtually impossible to argue with someone who simply will not argue back. And once you offer a spirit of possibility, creative solutions almost always present themselves.

Bill Ferguson, author of *How to Heal a Painful Relationship*, says, "You can be right or you can have love but you will never have them both." He claims that being right destroys love because it puts the other in the "wrong" category and stimulates resentment.

This habit is inspired by the Japanese martial art of aikido. Aikido is about redirecting the force of the attack rather than opposing it head on. In aikido, you use the attacker's momentum to turn his movement in a new direction.

This habit isn't about being a doormat and always saying yes. Instead, it invites you to examine whether you have the habit of chronic resistance—in other words, it encourages you to break a *bad* habit. Learning to change your pattern of conflict with a few simple words will lead to happiness.

Sam and Serena sat with their eyes closed. We were engaging in an exercise used by Daniel Siegel, the author of *Mindsight: The New Science of Personal*

Transformation. As per my instruction, Sam turned his body toward Serena and said the word, "No" out loud. Then he repeated the word "no" five more times, slowly, but with increasing intensity and tone. Then, in conclusion, he gently offered the word, "Yes."

As they opened their eyes, I asked Serena to reflect on how it felt to hear and receive the words. She said, "The 'no's' felt harsh, tense, almost scary. I could feel my heart start to beat a little faster when Sam got louder."

"And how was the 'yes' word for you?" I prompted.

"Totally different. Much softer, calmer," Serena replied.

What was true for Sam and Serena is true in a discussion between you and your spouse. The word "no," which most of us offer without even thinking twice, connotes strong negativity. While there may be occasions where a "no" is warranted, it is most often a knee-jerk reaction that deserves examination.

Serena had a history of saying no to Sam, of resisting his agenda and pushing her own. If he wanted to go out to dinner, watch a sporting event, leave his coat on the couch, read late to the kids—Serena's response was always "No, no, no." Her rules and expectations were rigid, and she was unaware of how much tension it was causing in their marriage.

After a month of agreeing to say, "Yes" as often as she could, Serena reported that she and Sam were getting along famously.

Serena reported, "I just say to myself, So what? Does it really matter? and then I say, Yes, sure."

Life is too short to always be on the defensive.

REFLECTION: What do you really gain by the need to always be right?

HABIT 39

Cushion

PROMPT: When you are going to knowingly disappoint your beloved

HABIT: Soften the blow with a "cushion." Lead your disappointing news with "I'm so sorry, but . . ." or "I'm so disappointed and I know you will be too, but . . ." Let your partner know that you recognize his feelings and/or wish it could be otherwise.

If you teach this habit to your spouse, you can ask for some cushion if he's disappointing you in a way that feels insensitive.

PURPOSE: When you couch potentially disappointing news in a way that indicates that you understand and honor your spouse's feelings, you soften the blow. You highlight the importance of your relationship in the face of imperfect circumstances. Disappointment is palatable if it is wrapped in regret and empathy. However, when disappointment is doused with disinterest, entitlement, and/or nonchalance, it is especially injurious. Developing the cushion habit lets your spouse know that he matters to you—always.

"All she said was, 'They called another meeting. I won't be home until late. *Don't* wait up for me.' And that's it. So much for family dinner night," Sam said.

Sam and Gillian had a nontraditional arrangement. Gillian was the primary breadwinner and Sam was the stay-at-home dad. He relished his role and loved being a "domestic engineer" (as he called it).

However, Sam often felt ignored and marginalized by Gillian. After three kids and fifteen years of marriage, he felt as if she took him for granted. She often had to stay late at work and even go on business trips at the last minute.

Gillian didn't particularly like having to work so hard, but her career offered a high salary. After she and Sam had their first child, they both agreed that it made sense for her to pursue her lucrative career in sales. He was happy to take care of the home front.

Gillian didn't mean to be unkind when she arrived home late night after night, but she was usually so stressed that she didn't consider the impact of her unexpected absences on Sam. She said, "Does he honestly think I enjoy working late? I hate it . . . especially if Sam is going to pout when I get home. I'd rather he just go to sleep without me."

I asked Gillian to try using the cushion habit the next time she encountered an unexpected schedule change. I suggested that she reach out to Sam and acknowledge how upsetting it must be for him. She was willing (even though she thought that Sam should be more empathic to her).

As it turns out, when Gillian softened her approach to Sam, he did the same. As Gillian explained how disappointed she was when her boss asked her to finish a report, and how she wanted more than anything to be home with Sam, Sam "heard" her. He heard that she was disappointed too.

Instead of punishing her with a cold dinner, as he might have in the past, he waited up and prepared her something fresh and warm to eat. They went to bed together, recognizing that they both wanted to feel close and connected in spite of the circumstances.

REFLECTION: Notice how when you take your lover's feelings into account, he tends to become more receptive and open to you.

HABIT 40

Zip It

PROMPT: When you feel the first flush of anger and realize that you're about to "lose it"

HABIT: Zip your lips, mentally count to ten, and then think of two different ways you could respond: with anger or with kindness. Even if your partner is being unreasonable or is intentionally trying to hook you, choose kindness.

PURPOSE: It's easy to stay with your old habit of being reactive. That response has become automatic, as if your spouse is determining your behavior. If you slow that process down by pausing just as you feel your anger rising, you will notice that there's always an ever-so-slight gap between the stimulus (what your spouse has said or done) and your response. In that gap, you can make a choice.

Spouses who adopt this habit learn to expand the gap. You can hold open that slight space in which you can make a choice about your reaction. In this gap lies the power between the high road and the low road, between habitual conflict and a happy marriage.

Rosemary had been working with me for about six months. She was particularly concerned about the ways in which her husband, Randy, pushed her emotional buttons. He had a way of blaming her for things that went wrong in his own life, and it drove her crazy. She always responded with anger.

Rosemary tried hard to be there for her husband but it always seemed to backfire on her. She packed his bags for business trips, but then he blamed her if he didn't have something he needed. She helped him keep track of his wallet, keys, and hat, but if they were misplaced, he was angry with her.

As part of her therapy, she spoke to him about giving him full responsibility for these personal aspects of his life. He agreed wholeheartedly and claimed he'd wanted more independence all along.

However, the first time he lost his keys he immediately marched up to her and said, "What have you done with my keys?"

Rosemary felt her face flush in anger and knew that was the cue to zip it. She counted to ten and then imagined saying either, "You're an irresponsible idiot! Figure it out," or "It must be frustrating to not be able to find them. Where's the last place you had them?" In the first option, she'd be belittling him; in the second, she'd be supportive. She chose the second course.

Over time, Randy became less accusatory and more self-reliant, a much healthier path for their interpersonal dynamic. Over time, they both learned the value of zipping it long enough to take the high road.

REFLECTION: What do you give up by not being reactive? What do you gain?

HABIT 41

Teamwork

PROMPT: After you have had an argument, and once you have calmed down. When it's time to "kiss and make up"

HABIT: Use a secret sign between the two of you that symbolizes, "We're a team. We're in this together. We love each other."

PURPOSE: The habit of repair is vital for minimizing long-term relationship deterioration. If you get into the habit of making sure that every altercation ends with a sense of togetherness, your marriage will stay strong.

Although how you handle a conflict matters (using "I" statements rather than "you" statements, and using respect rather than name calling), how you end the conflict is equally important. Fixing the connection after you have created a feeling of distance is essential for creating a happy marriage.

The use of a secret symbol is an intimate way to reconnect after discord or disappointment. As a habit, it reminds you that you are loving teammates and that your sense of connection is more important than the subject of your disagreement.

This habit is quite powerful. Once you've thoroughly integrated it into your behavior, you'll find that you use it frequently, both as a post-argument repair and as a way of strengthening your sense of unity.

I encourage every couple in my practice to create their own private, intimate teammate gesture. It might be a secret handshake, a dance step, or a series of touches. I've been quite impressed by the array of creative signs I've seen. While using your teammate symbol is a welcome habit for any occasion, it's especially vital after an argument to help you recalibrate.

Brian and Alexis had made quite a bit of progress in learning how to fight fair. That said, they still fought about what was best for their four-year-old daughter, Rebecca. Alexis, a stay-at-home mom, had very particular ideas about how Rebecca should be raised. She had a hard time letting Brian do things his way.

Brian had given Alexis a "day off," to spend with a girlfriend at a spa. Alexis had left Brian with a schedule detailing what Rebecca should eat, when she should nap, and what videos were appropriate for her to watch.

However, when Alexis came home she flipped. Rebecca hadn't napped, had eaten junk food, and had watched a football game with dad.

As she recounted that day in the session, her voice got louder. "Why couldn't he just do everything as I asked?" She was silent, and then she got teary-eyed. "Why am I the only grownup in the house?"

Brian looked shocked and opened his mouth to speak, but I intervened. "Alexis, do you believe that Brian loves his daughter?"

"Oh, I know that he does, but . . ."

"And do you think Rebecca will benefit from having a strong relationship with her daddy?" I continued. Alexis nodded.

I continued, "You can be a single parent making all the decisions on your own, or you can parent with Brian and learn from each other."

Alexis turned to Brian, "I know I get crazy controlling. I do want to parent with you."

Brian spontaneously reached his right hand for her left elbow. She responded by placing her left hand on his right elbow. This pretzel-armed gesture, I knew, was their "teammate" sign.

"We're in this together," Brian said. "Don't forget it."

REFLECTION: What do you gain by holding on to resentment? What do you gain by letting it go?

HABIT 42

Code Red

PROMPT: When you are out of control with your emotions

HABIT: Take a five- to fifteen-minute time out. Say, "I need a time out," or simply say "Code Red." Then go into another room to calm yourself down. Begin by counting ten exhalations; make them long and low in your body. Purse your lips as if you're blowing air through a straw. Next either splash cold water on your face, neck, and wrists, or count backwards from 100 by threes (100, 97, 94, 91, 88 . . .). Finally, when you feel more in control, return to your partner and say, "I'm ready to try again."

When you see that your partner is out of control, suggest, "I think we both need a time out." Before going into another room, explain that you will return in fifteen minutes but that it isn't productive to keep the conversation going under present conditions. Trying to converse with someone who is out of control is like trying to talk with an extremely drunk person. It doesn't work.

PURPOSE: When you get over-the-top upset, you are in what I call "code red." Your body is flooded by adrenalin and cortisol. The electrical signals from your limbic system (the emotional part of the brain) transmit two times faster than the electrical signals from the neocortex (the reasoning part of the brain). That means that you cannot think clearly because your body has kicked into the "fight/flight or freeze" response.

Taking a time out, much as giving one to a child who is having a tantrum, is a way to contain yourself until the storm passes. A series of deep and long exhalations is one of the quickest and most effective ways to stimulate the parasympathetic nervous system (the calming mechanism in the body). Splashing cold water on your face is a way to cool down the body, and counting backwards helps redirect the reactive mind. Both help you self-regulate (calm yourself down). Once you've reached a "code green," you're ready to try again.

Jennifer and Grant were a volatile couple. They frequently had dramatic shouting matches, which often resulted in tears, slammed doors, and occasionally shattered dishes. They were empty nesters now, and Jennifer was threatening to leave Grant if he couldn't get his anger under control.

To address this problem, I had taught them a system of alarm identification. If they were both in a reasonably calm state (code green), they could proceed with any discussion. However, if they saw signs of code red (shouting, screaming, slamming, sobbing), they needed to abort the discussion and take a time out. Most people also have a "code yellow," (warning, danger), but Jennifer and Grant tended to escalate to code red in a heartbeat.

They came into the session and Jennifer said, "I'm really at the end of my rope. We had a *gigantic* fight last Saturday. It exploded. Grant got drunk—he smashed a vase—and I nearly called the cops. I just don't see how we can go on." Grant hung his head.

"I agree that you shouldn't continue to have these scenes," I said. "Let's back it up. Tell me how it started."

Jennifer said they'd been arguing over whether to give their grown daughter some money for a down payment on a car. As their disagreement progressed, Grant told Jennifer that she was irresponsible with money, and then he began downing shots of tequila.

"So what did you do?" I asked Jennifer.

"I told him that he was a drunk, a lousy dad, and a cheapskate," she said.

"So you walked right into the storm, huh?" I replied. (This was shortly after Hurricane Sandy barreled up the eastern United States leaving devastation in its wake.) I explained to Jennifer that whenever she engaged in Grant's storms, rather than evacuating (taking a time out), she invited severe damage to herself, to him, and to their marriage. I explained to them about the code red habit and suggested they work on adopting it.

I don't know if Jennifer and Grant will be able to develop the habit of stopping a storm in its tracks, but I do know that the ability to evacuate, calm down, and start over is vital for the health of their relationship.

REFLECTION: It takes two people to whip up the conditions for a treacherous storm. Do you receive any benefit from the drama? Are you willing to end the escalation?

HABIT 43

Take Two

PROMPT: After an argument, preferably twenty-four hours after the conflict

HABIT: Sit down together and set a timer for ten minutes. Spend *up to* (but no longer than) ten minutes reviewing your recent argument. Analyze your own behavior by stating at least two ways that you could have handled the situation differently. Say, "I did this, but I could have done that" or "I said that, but I could have said this."

Try to be objective, as if you're critiquing a movie scene. This conversation is not about rehashing the topic, solving the problem, or discussing your feelings. The purpose is to deconstruct the pattern that occurs between you and determine how you contribute to that pattern (regardless of the topic). Dissect the interaction; define the point at which things escalated, and note where you began to act in a way that was reactive or when you began to shut down. When the ten minutes are up, end with a "Thank you for looking at this with me."

PURPOSE: You may notice that you and your mate get into the same argument over and over again. You could probably just play a tape recorder of the same old fight with the same old words that you've been saying for years. This habit inserts perspective into the cycle, creating the opportunity to develop a healthier pattern.

Like a performance review in which you assess your work and create new goals for yourself, this habit invites you to review your actions and learn from your mistakes. It is purposely limited to ten minutes so the conversation won't go on endlessly or spiral into another version of the previous argument.

After a conflict, you might be tempted to never mention that angry moment again. You may wish to sweep it under the carpet and ignore its impact. However, by doing so, you only reinforce its negative influence in your marriage.

When you make it a habit to review your *own* participation in an argument and see where you might have behaved differently, you increase the odds of breaking the cycle of repetitive, unproductive conflicts. While it may be tempting to point out how your partner behaved badly, keep the focus on yourself. Remember that you can't control or change your spouse's actions or insights. You can only work to improve your own behaviors.

Although Harrison and Caitlin were deeply in love, they found themselves reverting to immature, hurtful behaviors with each other. Each of them was guilty of name calling, yelling, and even throwing pillows at each other. Although they were both highly educated, they frequently acted like toddlers.

They came to see me because they wanted to start a family but were afraid to bring a child into a volatile marriage. Not surprisingly, Harrison felt that Caitlin needed to get a handle on her anger, while Caitlin felt that Harrison's immaturity was the core problem. In truth, the dynamic of their relationship was the culprit.

One week they came to see me, and Harrison announced that he had been sleeping in the guest bedroom for the past three nights. "What happened?" I asked.

Harrison announced dramatically, "Caitlin insulted me when I was late to the restaurant—she launched into an attack, actually, and I refuse to sleep in the same bed with her until she apologizes to me."

It's often the case that you feel you are owed an apology—and perhaps you are. However, you cannot *make* your spouse apologize to you. Blackmail or emotional extortion is not the answer.

In session, we untangled the feelings at the heart of this argument. Caitlin had felt abandoned when Harrison was late. Rather than voice her pain, she had lashed out. He reacted to her insults by shutting down. By talking about the argument, rather than the source of conflict, in just a few minutes Caitlin and Harrison were able to own their personal participation in the squabble and see how they could have handled things differently.

Happily they began sleeping in the same bed together that night.

REFLECTION: What happens to your marriage when you start focusing on how to improve your own actions, rather than focusing on what you think your spouse should do?

PART IV

Intimacy-Building Habits

You may think of intimacy as a synonym for sex, and to the degree that sex involves being naked, yes, sex has an intimate component. However, everyone knows that you can have sex with someone (physical connection) and not be particularly intimate (emotional connection). Likewise, you can be quite intimate with a friend but not be having sex with him or her.

There are all kinds of intimacies in life, but here we mean intimacy as a mutual unveiling with a partner. The word "intimacy," from the Latin root *intimus*, means "innermost." Intimacy with your spouse is a deep, openhearted connection in which you share your innermost self. Creating intimacy in your marriage dissolves the emotional, spiritual, physical, and sexual boundaries that keep you feeling lonely and disconnected.

True intimacy will create a new dimension in your marriage. By choosing to share each of yourselves authentically and openheartedly, you create an environment for rich growth and sublime love.

Remember that intimacy is a private affair between the two of you. In a happy marriage, intimacy is something that you share exclusively with your spouse. To the degree that you are this intimate with anyone else—particularly someone else of the opposite gender—you risk creating an "intimacy leak" in your marriage. Being unusually close to someone other than your spouse will begin to deflate the balloon of your marriage. So protect the intimacy you have with your spouse. Keep it exclusive, vibrant, and fresh.

Choosing to know and deeply accept another is an act of generosity. The great Jewish philosopher Martin Buber wrote, "The greatest thing one can do for another is to confirm what is deepest in another." This is the sort of mutual intimacy for which you should strive. This is the intimacy that your marriage deserves.

In this section of the book, you will discover habits that will help you share and receive each other sensually (Chapter 7), openheartedly (Chapter 8), and spiritually (Chapter 9).

CHAPTER 7

Sensory Spotlight: Habits for a Sensual Boost

"I just don't know what to do to feel close to her," said Jared. "We don't really have that many interests in common. I like to golf and she likes to be at the barn with her horses."

I listened and commented, "Perhaps it's more about *being* than about doing. You need to find ways to simply *be* together."

Jared expressed a sentiment that I hear over and over again. Couples may love each other, but they don't seem to know what to do with each other. You and your spouse may have gotten so wrapped up in the distractions of life that it's hard to imagine being close unless you've got an agenda. Or maybe you've both changed over time and the things that were fun in the past (like going to clubs or bars) no longer have the same appeal.

The five senses (sight, sound, smell, taste, and touch) act as a template for exploring the art of simply being together: no goals and no agenda other than feeling close and connected. Your marriage, unlike any other relationship in your life, has the potential to bring you the widest variety of sensually charged experiences, from simple touches, squeezes and hugs, sniffs and sounds, to highly erotic acts of bonding.

You and your spouse can use the following habits to stoke the fires of passion and ignite a sensational wordless communication of togetherness and love.

HABIT 44

Face It

PROMPT: If you're in bed, distracted from each other by a television or laptop

HABIT: Stop what you're doing and offer a face massage to your beloved. Rub her forehead, cheeks, nose, and chin. Massage her face, ears, and head tenderly and gently. Read her face as if you are reading Braille. Use your hand to gently stroke her face, almost as if your hand is a paintbrush, and you're painting on her face.

PURPOSE: The habit of intimate touching builds intimacy. When you engage in the loving power of touch, you make a connection. The face is an especially vulnerable and tender part of the body. Stan Tatkin, coauthor of *Love and War in Intimate Relationships*, uses a psychobiological approach to therapy and is fond of having couples "paint" each other's faces. He claims that it heightens a sense of trust and safety for the couple.

"So there we were in bed, next to each other, and we were both surfing the web on our separate laptops," said Cindy, an attractive woman in her thirties. She was seeing me for self-esteem issues. "So I said to Joe, 'Gosh, I haven't even seen you all day, and I missed you. Maybe we should spend some time together.'"

"That was a nice way to phrase it," I responded. "What did he say?"

She continued, "He said, 'What do you mean? This *is* spending time together.' And he looked back at his laptop. I didn't really know what else to say, so we just kept on doing our own things."

There are ways you can spend time together that involve intimacy and there are ways to spend time together that are more like parallel play. When you sit with your spouse with separate laptops, this falls into the category of parallel play.

Cindy shrugged it off, but I knew that when the habit of "separate time masquerading as time together" dominates a relationship, it leads to emotional distance. I suggested that she let her husband know that she wanted to spend a little time together more intimately and *then* they could sit side by side at their screens.

Touching the face has a private quality to it. I remember once being at a pool and watching a man sunscreening his female partner. It was noteworthy because he was gently sunscreening her face. He tenderly moistened her forehead, her nose, the delicate area above her lip, and her chin. Usually you might witness someone sun-screening a partner's back or shoulders, but not her face.

Judging by their behavior, they were a happy couple.

REFLECTION: How does your partner respond when you massage his or her face?

Slow Dancing

PROMPT: When you find yourself and your spouse getting undressed at the end of the day at the same time

HABIT: Say, "Wanna dance?" and then get up close, actually cheek to cheek, and take a few minutes for a teenage slow dance. Drape yourself on each other and sway from side to side. Let your feelings of love and connection be renewed. Option: Try slow dancing naked as a fun form of foreplay.

PURPOSE: Using this habit creates a memory of connection and safety as well as igniting an erotic, playful spark between you. When was the last time you had a private slow dance with your honey? Most of us may dance politely (and infrequently) at weddings but find no occasion to engage in "dirty dancing."

With or without music, slowly entangling your limbs and swaying to your internal rhythm joins the two of you into one. If you choose to do this naked, your skin, which contains more than 5 million sensory cells and is by far your largest sensory organ, gets a thorough stimulation.

Four middle-aged women were sitting in a café sipping cups of cappuccino and sharing stories about teenage children. Our children had grown up together, through the years of playgrounds, snow days, play dates, and later high school track meets and college applications.

One of us confided that she was feeling distant and lonely in her relationship with her husband, "When the kids were younger, we were so busy and distracted that we didn't notice how distant we were with each other. Now that the kids are older and out doing their own thing most of time, I'm feeling really disconnected from him."

This is a common phenomenon for middle-aged couples. The intimacy in your marriage can take quite a beating in competition with the demands of raising children. Years of "changing of the guard" can leave you feeling as if your spouse is more of a colleague than a love interest.

Cheryl, the oldest at the table, commented, "I remember feeling that way too. John and I had to make a real effort to come together again. I was worried that we wouldn't make it but after a real big fight, I think we both realized that we needed to make a change."

"About a year ago," Cheryl continued, "John and I both started making attempts to be romantic. I think we both had a sense that we were on the edge of a separation. I remember one night, when we were getting ready for bed, he hugged me and we started slow dancing. I just let down all my built-up defenses and we melted into each other. That dance was such a turning point for us."

"Now," Cheryl giggled, "John and I love to go up to our bedroom and slow dance like teenagers, dirty-dancing style."

It was rare that we shared information about our marriages. Looking back, I wish we had done so even more. We might have been able to learn more lessons from the success or failure of our marriages (two of us eventually divorced).

Cheryl was a shining inspiration to us. Now, almost a decade later, she and John are celebrating their twenty-fifth wedding anniversary. With the habit of regular slow dancing, I'm not surprised.

REFLECTION: What do you have to fear if you let yourself melt into a slow dance?

HABIT 46

Eye Candy

PROMPT: When you're feeling defensive or distant but are willing to have some help reconnecting

HABIT: You need some eye candy. Ask your husband or wife to sit quietly opposite you and then spend the next one to three minutes gazing into his or her eyes. Do not speak. Simply allow yourself to look into the windows of your lover's soul.

PURPOSE: Intensive eye contact communicates attraction, love, and trust. When you are attracted to someone, your pupils dilate and you hold their gaze. Prolonged eye contact stimulates feelings of affection and connection.

There is a primal basis for this visual comfort. Eye contact harkens back to your earliest attachment experience—the one you had with your primary caregiver. Infants depend on eye contact to receive a message of recognition, safety, and understanding from their caregiver.

When you gaze into your partner's eyes, you will discover a powerful jolt of intimacy. Even just a few minutes of this on a regular basis will create a sense of connection and of homecoming that restores your bond.

Because prolonged eye contact requires mutual trust, you may experience a feeling of discomfort in your first attempts. This is perfectly normal. Let yourself laugh with your spouse. The feeling of reconnecting may feel too deep and tender. Don't be surprised if it even brings tears. Eventually, this habit will bring a smile.

I once saw a woman for a consultation session regarding her grief over the death of her mother. However, rather than use the session to describe her feelings of loss, she instead complained nonstop about her husband. I suggested that she might need marriage counseling more than grief counseling. She decided to bring her husband with her for the next session. When they arrived, Joe appeared relaxed. I welcomed him and commented that making the decision to embark on marriage counseling was a brave step. "Marriage counseling?" he said, visibly tightening. "Jean didn't say anything about that. I thought I was just here to support her grieving."

Oops. I had just unwittingly participated in a complete ambush. Joe thought he was supporting Jean's sadness only to discover that their marriage was at stake. Over the next fifteen minutes he got increasingly defensive. Nothing was wrong with their relationship, he told me, and besides, he didn't know how to do any better. He assured me that forty-four years of marriage meant they were fine.

I tried to reframe the issue. "Her request for marriage counseling is a supreme compliment to you," I said. "Her primary goal is to feel closer to you. That's how much she loves you. Even after all these years together, she just wants to feel close to you."

He hung his head down. "I thought we *were* close. What else can I do?"

I suggested that they try an exercise right here in my office. I asked them to turn toward each other and just gaze into each other's eyes . . . for three minutes. Now, three minutes may not sound like a long time, but it can feel that way.

At first they were awkward and began to giggle. As they let go of their defenses, their shoulders dropped and a shift occurred. By the end, both of them had teared up. The transition from defensiveness to tenderness was a beautiful thing to witness.

When the time was up, he reached for her hand and said, "Honey, tell me what to do."

She smiled and brushed away a tear. "Thank you, Joe. You just did it."

Let intentional eye contact cut through your work, your distance, your resistance, and bring you closely toward each other. It's a habit that will carry your marriage forward with intimacy.

REFLECTION: Are you afraid to let yourself be fully seen?

HABIT 47

Mind's Eye

PROMPT: If you're feeling distant from your beloved

HABIT: Visualize a wonderful scene between you and your dear one. Imagine yourselves on your honeymoon, on a wonderful trip, relaxing in retirement, having a romantic dinner, walking on a beach, or even skinny-dipping! Hold your attention on this image and let yourself take in the details. Let the emotions and sensations that arise soak into your body.

PURPOSE: Creative visualization is an effective stress reliever. Conjuring scenes of intimacy and connection redirects the emotional responses of your mind and body. Visualization differs from daydreaming in that it is intentional and much more focused.

When you imagine yourself interacting with your spouse (relational visualization), it becomes more than just a sweet or sexy backdrop. This type of visualization activates the energy between you. Choose to relive a magical time with your mate; see it in vibrant detail and summon a feeling of togetherness to open your heart. Visualization is a natural mood booster. Let it boost your feeling of love.

I grew up in the suburbs. My experience with swimming was confined to a crowded country club. If it had occurred to me to skinny-dip—which it didn't—I probably would have been arrested.

Daniel, however, grew up on a farm in rural New Hampshire. He was so accustomed to secluded ponds that it didn't occur to him to wear a swimsuit! He was truly astonished when he learned that I had never gone skinny-dipping.

It was on our honeymoon in Bali that I discovered, in a private pool in a private villa, that skinny-dipping is truly fantastic! Who knew that a bathing suit was so restrictive? The natural feel of water on skin and . . . well, let's just say that skinny-dipping with your lover offers a unique feeling of fun.

One evening, years later, I was feeling unusually exhausted after a long day. I was also annoyed with Daniel because he had agreed to take care of a project that day but had forgotten to do so. I was feeling distant and alone.

Still, I didn't want to feel irritated. I wanted to enjoy my evening at home feeling relaxed. So I closed my eyes and went back to Bali. In my mind's eye I saw myself skinny-dipping with Dan. I could feel the water, the buoyancy, the freedom. I imagined riding along Dan's back as he chartered me through the waters. I felt the warmth of sun on my shoulders and the way that Dan laughed when I blew into his ear.

I became so engrossed in the visualization that I began to feel better in spite of myself. When I joined Dan for dinner, I was in a place where I could connect with my husband with gratitude and grace.

REFLECTION: Do you continue to create new memories together that might serve as a future visualization?

Spoonful of Sugar

PROMPT: Whenever you're having a decadent sweet treat together

HABIT: Take your fork or spoon and feed your spouse a bite of the delicious dessert. Alternately, hand feed your darling a small piece of food, letting your finger linger on his lips.

PURPOSE: The habit of feeding your lover will induce a sensual intimacy between you and a playful connectivity in your marriage. This habit is fun, sexy, and even seductive. And yet, how often do you ever feed your mate? Chances are that you haven't fed your loved one a piece of cake since the day you said, "I do."

Feeding your spouse is a nourishing, intimate act packed with sensual potential. Use it on a date night or just over coffee and chocolates to bring your marriage to a higher level of happiness.

The brochure boasted a Turkish feast for the senses, a once-in-a-lifetime romantic adventure that would surpass your wildest dreams. A tall order, to be sure, but the exotic spa had fulfilled its promise.

We had been whisked through an enticing and mysterious labyrinth: lush colors, exotic music, fabric walls, flowers, incense, jeweled statues, scarves draped from the ceiling. It was like a dream.

We were plunged into cool baths and hot baths. We were slathered in yogurt and had our faces covered in cucumber slices. We were kneaded and pummeled and rubbed down. And now Dan and I, honeymooners, were soaking together in a private basin, more swimming pool than tub. Toe to toe we floated, melting into the hot water strewn with rose petals and essential oils. Sandalwood incense filled the room. We felt like Turkish royalty.

A knock on the door heralded the arrival of a tray featuring cool mint tea and an assortment of Turkish delights. As I floated over to this plate of refreshments, Daniel selected one and fed it to me. The intimacy and love in that single act lifted me out of my separate world of physical pleasure and pulled us together in a way that all the luxury in the world could not. That small act of feeding brought us together as one.

Feeding your spouse a small bite is not just for weddings and honeymoons. It is a habit for ordinary living. Make it playful; make it romantic; make it sensual.

REFLECTION: What feeling arises within you when you let yourself be fed?

HABIT 49

Sounds of Silence

PROMPT: When you're too tired for words

HABIT: Say, "Let's listen together." For a set period of time (one to three minutes) simply listen together in silence. If it feels comfortable, hold hands. Close your eyes and *listen* to the array of sounds in the world around you. When thoughts come into your mind, simply redirect your attention back to the sounds. At the end of the time, share what you heard: the ticking clock, your beloved's breathing, cars going by.

PURPOSE: When you and your spouse develop the habit of taking a few minutes to come together in the present moment, you will find common ground and create a space where you can really connect. While listening to the details that surround you, you will experience a mental pause, a reprieve from the spiral of your stressful thoughts.

This habit is particularly great for coming together after work or before going to bed (or anytime you feel as if you and your spouse are in separate worlds). Listening mindfully has the effect of quickly recharging your energy. Be sure to end after the duration you agreed upon. A kitchen timer is perfect for this.

Daniel and I went on a silent retreat together, a bucolic country farm estate run by an order of Episcopalian monks. As we settled into our own private "hermitage" and prepared to go into silence, I eagerly anticipated our mutual stillness.

Almost immediately, though, I found the experience completely maddening. There was no way to communicate. How were we going to structure our time together? Dan looked calm as the Buddha himself. I found myself getting frustrated. As we sat on our sun porch in stony silence,

I thought, "This is like a dysfunctional marriage. Tons of couples never speak, and that doesn't make them happy. It makes them lonely and isolated." I continued to pout.

I *hated* the silence. It was as if I was experiencing the stillness as a kind of emotional abandonment. I couldn't stand it.

Then Dan caught my eye, took my hand, and made a gesture that plainly meant, "Let's take a walk." On that walk, in total silence, we listened to the world together. We heard honking geese fly nearby, so low that we could see the whites of their bellies. Dan pointed out autumn leaves rustling on the ground. I called his attention to chipmunks skittering across fallen logs. We found a hammock that held the two of us side by side and spent the next hour listening to the sounds of the world. I no longer felt alone because I knew that we were listening together.

I'll admit that twenty-four hours is a long time to be silent. But intentional listening together only takes a few minutes. This habit allows you both to travel from your separate worlds of nonstop thinking to your home together in the here and now. Listen to the sounds of life with your beloved and share in the wonder of your world together.

REFLECTION: Is there anything that you're afraid you will "hear" if you allow yourself to rest in silence?

HABIT 50

Listen to This

PROMPT: When your partner is complaining

HABIT: Breathe deep and listen. Do not try to fix, minimize, defend against, or deny his feelings. Instead, listen until he is done and then say, "What I hear you saying is . . ." Then paraphrase his words. Continue by saying, "Did I get that right?" and "Is there more?"

PURPOSE: As you develop the habit of listening when your husband or wife needs to complain, you will find that conflict and stress in your marriage will decrease. Unless your spouse has asked for a solution to his problem, you can be sure that when he complains he simply needs to feel heard.

This mirroring tool is inspired by Harville Hendrix's "Intentional Dialogue" exercise in Imago Relationship Therapy. This structured way of listening helps your partner feel understood and prioritized.

When you listen without judgment or the desire to redirect, you are able to offer empathy and reception. This heartfelt presence to the experience of our beloved offers the gift of acceptance. John Gray, author of *Why Mars and Venus Collide: Improving Relationships by Understanding How Men and Women Cope Differently with Stress*, points out that for women this is especially important. When a woman feels like she is heard and supported, her oxytocin levels rise, allowing her to feel calm and relaxed.

If you are busy constructing your own comeback to your spouse's complaints, you are not able to hear her words or empathize with her feelings. Let this directed technique of listening become a habit, and you will have a greater feeling of understanding infuse your marriage.

Jennifer had a long list of complaints when she came in with her husband Nate. They had been married for six years and had two young children. Both Jen and Nate worked full-time jobs and were overwhelmed with the demands of a busy family life.

"After dinner, Nate refuses to help me clean up the dishes," Jennifer complained.

Nate shook his head and sighed, "She's got it all wrong. I tell her that I'll help, but I want to do it after the kids go to bed. Is that so wrong? She's so controlling about it."

"Really? I tried that and you left the dishes in the sink for two days!" Jen countered. "I don't want to live in a pigsty. Why can't you just help around the house? Do you think I'm your maid? Besides, I want to be with the kids too, you know." Her tone was biting.

I interjected. "It sounds like both of you really want something that you just can't quite get." I wanted to break the rhythm of the argument, so I told them about the mirroring exercise. I asked Jen to listen in this specific way, while Nate talked.

Jen listened to Nate repeat his feelings about kitchen cleanup. Then she summarized his feelings: "What I hear you saying is that it's important to you to spend some fun time with the kids before they go to sleep. You don't want to blow that time cleaning up the kitchen."

Next, Nate listened to Jen and mirrored back: "What I hear you saying is that it's important to you to have the kitchen cleaned up before we go to bed. You don't want to wake up to a dirty kitchen. And, you also want to spend time with the kids before they go to sleep."

Yes. Exactly. Once they both felt heard, they suddenly dropped their frustrated, sarcastic tone. And in the space of open dialogue and a mutual goal, a solution arose. They decided to clean the kitchen together at 8 P.M., after putting the kids to bed. Jen dropped her need to clean the kitchen at 6 P.M. and Nate dropped leaving the cleaning until the next day. Both of them got to spend time with the kids.

Not every solution presents itself so clearly, but one thing is for certain: If you don't *listen* to each other, you won't find your way. So try to get into this habit. You may be surprised by what you hear.

REFLECTION: Are you willing to stop and listen to your spouse even when *you* wish to be heard?

Air Freshener

PROMPT: When you see that your beloved is standing at the kitchen sink washing the dishes, or—if she's not often at the sink—whenever she's doing any chore

HABIT: Go over and nuzzle into her neck. Inhale deeply. Kiss in her neck and/or at the nape of her neck and say, "Thank you."

PURPOSE: Appreciative neck nuzzling is a gratitude habit that offers recognition and affection to your partner in life. Gratitude has the enormous power to bring smiles, joy, and intimacy into your marriage.

Neck nuzzling also activates an olfactory sensory experience that enhances couple bonding. The neck, like the wrists and behind the ears, is a pulse point. This physical repository of blood vessels close to the skin acts as a fragrance pump and offers each person's unique scent to the one willing to snuggle close.

All mammals secrete pheromones, chemicals that trigger sexual and social responses in members of their own species. Many researchers believe that for humans, too, an individual's sexual and social behavior is affected by the odorless pheromones secreted by individuals with whom they have intimate contact. Nuzzle up to your spouse's neck and let yourself bond with the one you love.

Dan and I were at a couples yoga retreat. We were learning the ancient art of Thai yoga, a partner-based stretching yoga. The instructor taught a series of poses—part massage, part stretch, and part snuggle. Each couple was on a futon mattress to learn the various poses.

During the opening session, we had each introduced ourselves, saying how long we had been partnered and why we were taking this weekend workshop. Each couple offered a unique story of love and commitment to improving their relationship.

There was the elderly couple who were celebrating their forty-sixth wedding anniversary. Over there was the lesbian couple on the verge of breaking up, who hoped that this retreat together would build their bridge back to connection. Right next to us was the touchy-feely young couple who had never tried yoga before. And across the way was the couple who had just launched their last child to college and found themselves in rediscovery mode.

I got up from our futon mattress to go to the bathroom. Strangely, as I did so, I had to step over couples lying on their own futons. These couples were in various stages of spooning, hugging, cuddling, and holding. It was as if I had landed in a huge slumber party . . . except everyone was adult, coupled, and physically attached.

It was the newly empty nester couple who most caught my attention. The husband was gently nuzzling the neck of his long-time bride. It was such a sweet, intimate moment that I must have blushed as I averted my gaze.

Over the next few days, what I noticed most was the frequent nuzzling behavior amongst those couples who seemed the happiest. It was as if happy couples unconsciously verified and intensified their bond through the tactile and olfactory experience of nuzzling with each other.

REFLECTION: Can you nuzzle your partner's neck even if you're feeling annoyed or downhearted? Can you give even when you don't feel like it?

HABIT 52

Coming Up Roses

PROMPT: When you want to increase your experience of joy with your partner

HABIT: Notice what you are doing together and inhale sharply. As you inhale, think or say the words, "I breathe in this moment and notice its beauty." Exhale slowly and let the good feelings sink into your body.

PURPOSE: When you make it a habit to breathe in the beauty of the small enjoyable moments of your relationship, you increase your own capacity for mindfulness, happiness, and joy.

Mindfulness is a practice of nonjudgmental awareness that increases your ability to savor and experience the present moment. You've probably heard the expression "Stop to smell the roses." That's mindfulness in practice. Neuroscience has shown that mindfulness exercises, such as this habit, help to reduce stress and increase one's happiness level.

Deep breathing is also known to ground you in your body and ground you in the moment. Breathing in an experience is doubly powerful.

Sarah, a forty-six-year-old mother of two, married for twenty years, shook her head as she told me, "I just wish I could feel more joy with Ron. Everything feels so ordinary."

"Do you do things together that you enjoy?" I asked.

"I suppose so," she responded. "Do you mean like hobbies and stuff?"

"No, not necessarily," I answered. "I mean, do you simply enjoy his company, enjoy your life with him?"

I explained to Sarah that perhaps it was possible that she was looking in vain for million-dollar moments and mountaintop highs to bring her joy. "The reality is that your relationship primarily consists of simple, seemingly ordinary moments. You just have to realize how extraordinary these moments really are."

I asked her to keep a journal with her throughout the day and list everything that she enjoyed. Did she like her morning coffee, exchanging e-mails with a friend, and hugging her daughter when she came home from work? Did she enjoy sharing a glass of wine with her husband, listening to him discuss his day, watching him read their son a bedtime story?

When she returned the next week she marveled that there were, in fact, dozens of moments every day that she relished. Then I suggested this habit to her. She came back the following week beaming. When she'd let herself breathe in these moments she'd identified, she told me, they somehow felt bigger and more special.

"I'm happier than I realized," she quipped. "Who knew life was so good?"

The wise Buddhist nun, Pema Chödrön, suggests that happiness is a *habit*. Once you develop the art of noticing goodness, you start to see it everywhere. Applying this to your relationship allows you to see even the smallest interactions with reverence. The simple task of eating scrambled eggs in the morning with your mate suddenly becomes a quiet cause for celebration.

A happy marriage is built upon the little things. Breathe in the beautiful daily moments and feel your marriage come to life.

REFLECTION: When do you feel most alive in your relationship?

HABIT 53

Candlelight Night

_____

PROMPT: Once per season, perhaps on the solstice or the equinox

HABIT: Have a planned sensual and sexual evening in bed with no television, no books, just each other. Plan to light candles, play music, wear lingerie, bring lotion, or use sex toys. The point is to explore and take your time . . . have an evening where you linger over each other's body parts and reconnect with every sense.

PURPOSE: Happy couples have sex. In fact, sex is the ultimate exclusive activity that you share with your spouse and only your spouse. While you can love and even feel deeply attached to other people in your life, you are only (or should be) having sex with your spouse.

It is not uncommon for a busy couple to drop sex as a priority. As with exercise, you might know that you "should," but you just don't have the energy. That's why it's important for you to schedule a sexual liaison and give yourself time to enjoy it (which means going to bed long before you're actually tired and ready to fall sleep).

Having regular sex is a natural, healthy, and important habit in a healthy marriage. It is a crucial component in the human need for physical _and_ emotional closeness, connection, and intimacy. It releases chemicals in your brain that relieve stress and help you feel connected.

Many couples find it odd, at first, that I'd recommend scheduling sex since it seems the antithesis of spontaneous passion. However, the benefits are immense. For men, scheduled sex offers a relaxed, no-rejection anticipation as well as a willingness for a romantic buildup. For women, a longer sensual evening offers more satisfaction than a "quickie" and lets her know that she is prioritized.

Are you frequently overwhelmed and stressed by a life that includes children and stressful jobs? Has having sex become one more chore on your to-do list, something to squeeze in between flossing and folding laundry? Is it quick, rote, dull, and meaningless? Or has it even become obsolete? If you feel like you're living with a roommate, you are not unlike millions of others in virtually sexless marriages. This habit will help turn things around.

In the film *Hope Springs*, a marriage counselor (actor Steve Carell) asks a couple (Meryl Streep and Tommy Lee Jones) when they last had sex. The husband claims not to remember. The wife knows right away that it was four years ago.

Unfortunately, when you cool down the sexual side of your marriage, it can be difficult to reignite it. Then, even when kids grow up and the job stress lessens, you find that you either don't want or don't know how to restart a happy sex life with your spouse.

In an effort to jump-start the passion between his clients, Carell asks them to first just hold each other for an evening, then to touch each other, then to share their sexual fantasies, and finally to have sex. The tender rebuilding of a physical relationship between the couple is at times both painful and hilarious to witness. But they do find their way back to each other and to a physical connection.

The movie champions the message that it's never too late to change your habits of physical intimacy. In intentionally creating the seasonal habit of a sensual evening together, you will bring a new level of romantic anticipation into your marriage as well as a deeper satisfaction to your sexual experience.

REFLECTION: Are you willing to honor and prioritize a sexual relationship with your spouse?

CHAPTER 8

People Will Say We're in Love: Habits to Open Your Hearts

People everywhere want nothing more than to be coupled. Marriage is seen as the ultimate interpersonal commitment, the holy grail of relationships. You long for it, strive for it, wish for it, pray for it and then—pow! It happens to you. You want the happiness to last, of course. You want the love to be forever.

But love is tricky. On the one hand, when you are at your best, it means caring about your partner's needs more than your own, giving with an open heart. On the other hand, romantic love often implies some expectation of return, some measure of reciprocal devotion.

Conditional love means, I love you as long as . . . you stay thin, get rich, tell me what I want to hear, don't do anything that will force me to hate you, and frankly, as long as I feel like it. On the other hand, unconditional love—the love you might experience regularly with your pets or your children—means I love you even when you change, even when I change, even when you have a tantrum, even when you're rude to me, even when I don't feel like it, because my heart is large and open.

When it comes to true, unconditional love, the love in your marriage has its source *within* you. You can't control your spouse's capacity for unconditional love but you can model it for him or her. It's a measure of your capacity for a big, open heart. Think of the well-known Dr. Seuss furry Christmas creature, the Grinch. When he hears the Whos down in Whoville still singing even though their Christmas had been stolen, his heart grows to three times its size.

You might find it easy to act in loving ways when you *feel* loving, but what about when you don't feel that way? Amazingly, it is possible to act "as if." Your emotions will respond to your actions: When you act in loving ways, you start to feel loving. The habits in this section are designed to open your heart, to help you act in loving ways so that you feel loving as a result. Keep your heart open and love will bloom.

HABIT 54

Full Cup

PROMPT: When you get dressed in the morning

HABIT: Stop for a moment and cradle your face by placing your hands on your cheeks. Repeat these words out loud: "May you be happy. May you be healthy. May you be safe from harm. May you know peace. You are a wonderful person. You deserve love."

Hint: In a place where you will see it, keep a Post-it with these words (or others that resonate for you) until you have them memorized.

PURPOSE: This habit is about filling your own cup with love and happiness. You—and nobody else—are responsible for your own happiness. You don't need to look for another person to complete you, as if you were faulty or only half of a person. No, you are completely whole on your own. Your beloved partner merely makes you more whole and happier.

John Gray, relationship expert and author of *Men Are from Mars, Women Are from Venus*, proclaims that individuals are responsible for 90 percent of their own happiness. A person's partner can help top off the extra 10 percent.

The words in this habit are based on the Buddhist meditation known as the *Metta Bhavana* (a practice of loving kindness). Most people don't offer themselves love and compassion. Decide to become your biggest and best cheerleader. When you fill your mind with this kind of loving, positive self-talk, you will dwell in love and your cup will runneth over.

The gesture of cradling your face adds to the sense of tender self-love and triggers your instinctual caretaking.

In order to truly love another person, you have to begin with yourself. This was the lesson that my client Charlotte finally learned. Charlotte and Gene had been married for three years. They came to see me because Charlotte was obsessed with the fear that Gene was going to leave her.

Although Gene was a kind and gentle husband, his words of love and endearment often fell on deaf ears. He told her that she was beautiful, but she didn't believe it. He told her that he adored her, but she figured it wouldn't last. She often said in session that she didn't understand why someone as wonderful as Gene would fall in love with someone as mediocre as herself.

Gene shook his head in frustration. "No matter what I say, it's not enough," he said. "I can't convince her that she's wonderful. I don't know what to do to help her."

I recognized that Charlotte's lack of self-love was getting in their way. If she didn't change her ability to feel lovable, the trajectory for their marriage was in jeopardy.

"I believe that Charlotte needs to do some inner work on her own," I interjected. "Gene, you can support her but, ultimately, you cannot do this work for her."

As the months unfolded, Charlotte bravely looked at her childhood, investigated her internalized messages, and opened herself to being in the world in a new way. She was willing to do the "Full Cup" exercise every day until it became habitual, because she didn't want to lose Gene and she wanted to feel like a whole person.

I noticed that, as time went by, she began to smile more, to reach out to Gene in sessions, and to speak positively about herself. I knew that it was time to end our work together when Charlotte could receive Gene's love, know that she deserved it, and give it back in abundance.

REFLECTION: How could your marriage improve if you lived a life grounded in self-love?

HABIT 55

Heartstrings

PROMPT: When you're separated from your beloved in a social situation—a party, a gathering, a large crowd

HABIT: Make eye contact with your partner and discretely tug on your earlobe.

PURPOSE: It's easy to feel distant from your honey when you're surrounded by a group of people. As you make eye contact and tug on your ear, this private and physically intimate sign will instantly connect you and remind you that you love and are loved.

This famous earlobe tug was covertly introduced in 1967 during the CBS variety hour, *The Carol Burnett Show*. Carol ended every show with the same song and a tug on her earlobe. It was a private "I love you" sign meant for her grandmother who had raised her.

Once your sweetheart knows the meaning of the sign, she'll be assured that she's at the center of your heart, even when surrounded by a crowd.

It wasn't that Rosa disliked Miguel's family. In fact, she really loved her mother-in-law and the entire gang of Miguel's siblings, spouses, and their children. His four brothers, with their wives and children, made up a rowdy crowd of twenty-four people.

However, Rosa complained to me, "Whenever we go over there for dinner, Miguel ends up with his brothers playing pool for hours. I get stuck in the kitchen preparing food with all the other women. The kids run around like wild animals. I enjoy the evenings in some ways, but I never feel close to Miguel. In fact, it seems like he hardly notices me."

I suggested that she tell him about this sign and then use it several times during the evening. She told me that she wished that he would be the one to use the sign for her, because he was the one who seemed to ignore her. I explained to her that she couldn't necessarily change his behavior but she could focus on her own. Sometimes when you *become* the change that you wish, you *create* the change that you wish.

The next time I saw Rosa, she smiled demurely. "The first time I tried using the sign, it didn't seem to register. But then I did it again, and I got such a beautiful smile from Miguel. After that, he used it for me!"

"It was a subtle shift," she continued, "but it was fun and made a real difference. I felt better about the evening with his family. Maybe those parties aren't so bad after all."

REFLECTION: Are you willing to initiate the change that you desire?

HABIT 56

Angel Wings

PROMPT: When your partner seems sad, tired, or anxious

HABIT: Sit next to your spouse and sync up your breathing. Do this by putting your hand on his back or his belly. Notice the pattern of his breathing and then start to match the rhythm with your own breathing. Spend a few moments breathing together. At the end of this experience, kiss your partner tenderly and softly on his eyelids, first one eyelid and then the other.

PURPOSE: This habit is like a lifeline when your spouse is feeling adrift. Gay and Kathlyn Hendricks, authors of *Conscious Loving*, advise that couples intentionally breathe together on a regular basis. The simple act of matching your partner's breathing, they say, changes your state of consciousness. It creates a real but magical energy between you.

Kissing the vulnerable and tender spot of your spouse's eyelid actually stimulates your body in a way that contributes to feeling bonded. The combination of touching, breathing, and kissing creates a sense of emotional safety and spiritual grounding.

Quincy and Mariah had only been married for three years when they came to see me. They had been trying to have a baby during that entire time but to no avail. In fact, even though Mariah was only thirty-five, she had a long history of gynecological issues. The last blow had just occurred when Mariah was recently advised to have a hysterectomy.

Clearly their dream of conceiving a baby was now over. They told me they weren't interested in adoption. Instead they wanted to adjust to the reality that they would not have children.

As they described their situation to me, Quincy looked dazed. Mariah began to cry softly, looking increasingly more distressed. Quincy threw up his hands as he gazed at her, saying, "There's nothing I can do."

I said simply, "Actually, there is."

"But I can't change our circumstances," he countered.

"No, but you can provide emotional support, which is what she needs most," I advised. "You can be there for her, a loving presence, so she knows she isn't alone."

Mariah began crying harder now, saying, "He doesn't know how to do that."

I instructed Quincy, "If you're willing, could you put your hand on her back? I want you to feel her breathing."

He was willing and so we spent the next few minutes with Quincy cueing in to her breathing, which went from ragged and shallow to deep and slow. By the time he offered her kisses on her eyelids as per my direction, she had calmed down considerably. She, in turn, felt spontaneously moved to kiss his eyelids.

I summarized, "That's what you can do . . . no matter what the circumstances."

REFLECTION: Are you willing to be there for your spouse, to comfort her, even when you cannot change your circumstances?

HABIT 57

Heart to Heart

PROMPT: If you're starting to feel distant from your mate

HABIT: Put your hand on your beloved's heart and ask her to put her hand on your heart. Then hum a note and have your spouse hum it with you, matching the tone. Hum together until one of you changes the note. Match again and hum.

PURPOSE: When you feel distant from your spouse, this simple habit will quickly realign you and make you feel connected. Touching each other over the heart stimulates the bonding hormone of oxytocin.

Sharing the same sound waves creates a frequency of connection. Sound vibrates through your cells and unites you in a common vibration. Making a habit of joining through sound and touch reminds you that you are together in life and that your marriage is a priority.

I sat with a group of three middle-aged women over lunch, all of us already or close to being empty nesters, or, as I like to say, free birds. One had just launched her final child and was marveling at how much time she and her husband were spending together.

Hillary lowered her voice and confessed, "You all know that Rick and I were sort of drifting from each other the past couple of years. We were just so busy with the kids and our careers . . . but luckily, neither of us strayed outside the marriage. Now that it's just the two of us again, we realize that we really do love each other."

I've heard it said that having children is like throwing a hand grenade into a marriage. Being a parent is wonderful and is obviously extremely important for the propagation of the species, but it can turn a happy marriage upside down. When distracted by the labor-intensive work of raising children, you have to be especially mindful as a couple to keep your connection a priority (and that's where the 75 habits can help!).

Some couples find their way back to each other when their nest is empty, but sadly, other couples get lost and never reconnect.

"What kind of things are you doing together?" I probed.

Hillary smiled mischievously, "We're having sex again!" The three of us cheered. "And we're playing tennis together. Oh, and we're humming together."

"Humming?" we asked in unison.

"I guess because Rick is a music teacher, you know, but he just started humming to me and then, one day, I hummed back. Now we stand close to each other and take turns matching notes," Hillary said sheepishly. She continued, "I wish we had thought to do this years ago. If only he had hummed to me when the kids were growing up, I might not have felt so lonely. I know it sounds silly but when we match tones, I can sort of feel myself getting in sync with him."

"What a great idea," I said. "Try putting your hands on each other's hearts while you hum. Touch and sound together are an amazing combination."

We all agreed to go home and try this new habit. Dan and I have been using it together ever since.

REFLECTION: Are you willing to be the one to initiate connection, even when you're feeling distant from your spouse?

HABIT 58

Penny

PROMPT: When you or your darling is sitting in silence and you'd like to start a conversation

HABIT: Say "penny" (as in, "for your thoughts"). Your spouse should say immediately what he or she was just thinking and be uncensored and honest. Hear this true answer, whatever it may be.

PURPOSE: You want your beloved to know you . . . and you want to know his or her deepest thoughts as well. When you cultivate the habit of inquiring about your spouse's inner world—and sharing your world in return—you come to know each other better. Intimacy is built on the idea of sharing yourselves with each other.

Caring enough to be interested in your mate's thoughts is an attractive quality. Demonstrating that you care, and that you're willing to hear the true answer, indicates your commitment to your marriage.

A prerequisite to this habit, of course, is feeling emotionally safe with your spouse. Your partner needs to feel sheltered in order to truly share and reveal himself. Likewise, you also need to feel safe to be receptive and giving. All of the habits in this book are about building that emotional safety with your spouse.

Regina told me her husband complains that he never knows what she's thinking. He says that she's hard to read and never shares herself with him.

"Is that true?" I asked her. "Are you intentionally not talking with him about certain issues or feelings?"

"Well actually . . . yes," she answered. "Even though I know I should be able to tell him anything, I feel embarrassed. Maybe he doesn't want to know what's really on my mind."

"Are you willing to play a game to help him know what you're thinking? I think it will help the two of you get closer. He obviously wants to know you better and know what you're really feeling," I said.

We discussed the "Penny" habit, and she agreed to try it.

The next week she came in to report that the game was a huge success.

"I feel like we're getting to know each other on a whole new level," she said, blushing.

"For both of us, we've never felt closer."

REFLECTION: Are you willing to be honest with your partner about your thoughts? Do you believe you have thoughts you need to hide? What is the cost for doing so?

HABIT 59

Phone Home

PROMPT: At night if you are in separate places and are having a phone conversation

HABIT: End the conversation with a "phone hug." You should both close your eyes and imagine yourselves in the same place, either standing or lying down. Tell your partner how it feels to hug him or her, what you feel and what you imagine. Picture yourself in that embrace. Take at least sixty seconds with this habit.

Although modern technology with Skype and FaceTime make visuals possible, this habit uses audio only and requires both of you to close your eyes.

PURPOSE: When you intentionally connect emotionally during a time of physical separation, you create a safety net for your relationship. You affirm your commitment to each other and to the health of your marriage.

Having your eyes closed helps you summon visual and sensual details in your imagination. You may or may not talk as you engage in this virtual hug, but either way, you'll be creating a sense of union that makes you feel closer . . . even when you're far apart.

Sharon's first husband, Jim, was a pilot. They had been married for nine years, and in all that time, she had never gotten accustomed to his frequent departures. After they had their first child, it got worse.

She complained that she was a "work widow." When he moved from the domestic route to the longer absences of an international route, she cried. However, over time, she learned not to react . . . and eventually, not to even notice. She began to dread his returns because she had learned to run the household so effectively without him.

When she learned he was having an affair in Tokyo, she filed for divorce with little emotion. She would always blame his career for her psychological withdrawal and for the death of their marriage.

Now, a decade later, with this emotional baggage in tow, I understood when Sharon cried hysterically upon learning that her second husband, Anthony, was going on a business trip. Not only did she feel abandoned, she believed this trip signaled the beginning of the end of her marriage.

I assured her it didn't need to be this way. She could put habits in place to ensure that she and Anthony stayed close even with miles between them.

"Did you ever talk on the phone with Jim when he traveled?" I asked.

"Oh, sure, he called every night. He asked about the kids, if he had received any mail, if I had paid the bills. You know, just ordinary chitchat," Sharon replied.

"Well I'd like you to try something different," I suggested. I told her about the "Phone Hug" habit. She said she would try it.

During our next session, Sharon reported that the phone hug had been a big hit. She described it as being kind of sexy. They had lowered their voices and described nuzzling into each other's necks and wrapping their arms around each other.

"It was almost spooky," she said, "I could literally feel a shiver down my spine just by imagining him next to me." She continued, "I still would rather he not travel, but emotional presence sure does make physical absence more tolerable."

REFLECTION: Are you willing to stay connected even when you are physically apart?

HABIT 60

Sticky Honey

PROMPT: When you're leaving on a trip (however short or long)

HABIT: Write a brief love note for your dear one and put it in a surprise place (in her lunch box, on the bathroom mirror, in the fridge, in a sock drawer, on her pillow, in a purse or briefcase, on her computer screen). Use just a few words (even "XO" can make an impact).

PURPOSE: When you write "honey notes" for your spouse to find when you travel, you offer her constant reminders of your love. Let your beloved know that even when you're separated, you are thinking of her and doing your best to nurture the marriage.

Little love notes are a gift to your spouse. According to Gary Chapman, author of *The Five Love Languages: The Secret to Love That Lasts*, gifts are one of the ways to communicate love. (He identifies five categories of love expression: touch, gifts, acts of service, quality time, and verbal affirmation.) If you adopt this habit, you'll ensure that your spouse feels treasured and cherished. Putting Post-its in surprising places also creates novelty and fun, thereby stimulating a small dose of dopamine (a feel-good brain chemical) for your mate.

Note: Alternately, if your spouse is going on the trip, you can put surprise love notes in her suitcase or bag.

"The real issue couples have in the twenty-first century is that they don't take the time to nurture their bond. Everything else takes priority," said the couples expert. She was a seasoned clinician teaching a group of forty mental health professionals about "Emotionally Focused Therapy" for couples.

She proceeded to tell us of a couple with whom she had just successfully ended treatment. She said, "I knew they really didn't need counseling any more when he told me that his wife leaves sticky love notes in his lunch box every day." Several people around me sighed.

"I know," our storyteller continued. "Can you imagine if I found a love note in my suitcase from my husband tonight? I would be so excited. I know he loves me but he just would never think to do that. I mean, who would?"

"Dan would," I thought. "Dan already did."

Dan always leaves sticky love notes in my suitcase if I travel without him. And if he travels without me, I find hidden notes all over the house—in my desk, in my purse, beside my toothbrush. He taught me, with just a few little scraps of paper, how sweet it is to feel valued and special.

Once you begin associating your suitcase and travel toiletries with a pen and pad of sticky notes, you'll easily develop this habit. The notes don't need to be elaborate or fancy—just a small way to let your honey know that he matters to you.

It's especially important for your spouse to feel like he's important to you when you're physically apart. As you travel, it's easy to get caught up and start to feel separate from your home life. This habit helps you stay connected even when you're divided. Let absence make the heart grow fonder (and not simply out of sight, out of mind).

REFLECTION: How connected do you feel when you are apart from your spouse?

HABIT 61

Baby Doll

PROMPT: When you greet each other and/or when you are together in the bedroom

HABIT: Use a pet name or nickname when you address your spouse. If you already use nicknames, try a new one. Some examples of common terms of endearment are sugar, good lookin', lover, sweetie pie, tiger, teddy bear, sexy lady, muscle man, sugar lips, baby doll, etc. Allow yourself to be creative and generously flattering. Consider coming up with sweet, silly, or complimentary words for "private parts" as well.

PURPOSE: When you develop the habit of playful nicknames in your relationship, you add a dimension of fun, spontaneity, and uniqueness to your marriage. If you already have some tried and true pet names for your spouse, this tool invites you to be intentional about changing things up and being freshly appreciative. Treat the "Baby Doll" habit as a game and see what sticks.

Drs. Charles and Elizabeth Schmitz, preeminent couples therapists, state in their book, *Building a Love That Lasts: The Seven Surprising Secrets of Successful Marriage,* that loving nicknames are almost a ubiquitous characteristic of happily married couples. They call nicknames a "private code for love." Every happy marriage has its own verbal and physical cues for "I love you." Secret pet names and public nicknames are one way to keep love flowing in your marriage.

Every couple is different in the degree to which they use playful names. Some only use them in private, others only in public. Some couples always use a nickname to refer to their spouse, while others use one only in the bedroom. You will be surprised how a new nickname will charge up the tender expression in your spouse's eyes.

Once during a visit to Tennessee, Dan and I were a bit startled when the waiter came to our table and said, "Okay, sugar bun and honey pie . . . what can I git y'all to drink?" After the waiter left, I asked, "Which one of us is honey pie?"

Dan laughed and said, "Hey, I'm not gonna let that waiter talk sweeter to you than I do . . . baby doll . . . honey lips."

For the rest of that trip, we adopted thick southern accents and developed increasingly creative terms of endearment for each other. Although pet names may seem, on the surface, rather ridiculous, they express fun, admiration, and love.

You'll need to find the right pattern for you, but one thing is for certain: When you use verbal codes to communicate the unique love you have for your spouse, your connection comes alive and the "us" space blossoms.

REFLECTION: Notice what energy begins to emerge when you become verbally playful with your spouse.

HABIT 62

Go Public

PROMPT: When you're with your spouse at a party or at a family gathering

HABIT: Compliment your spouse in his or her presence in public. Be generous and authentic in your praise.

PURPOSE: Your spouse wants to feel important and valued in your eyes. When you make a habit of complimenting your mate in front of other people, you publicly declare your admiration for her. Additionally, you strengthen your own ability to appreciate your mate. Finally, when you practice this habit in public, you model to others how happy couples behave.

The flip side of this, a deeply damaging habit for your marriage, is publicly insulting or humiliating your mate—even if it is in a teasing way. Every so-called "joke" has an element of truth. When you make fun of your spouse at a party or gathering, you weaken your bond.

Let others know you think your spouse is terrific. Let your children know you think your partner is amazing. Make your spouse feel cherished in a whole new way.

Richard and Suzanne wanted desperately to be closer to each other—they had simply lost their way. After twenty years of raising kids and advancing their careers, they had developed habits of distance and independence.

Suzanne claimed that she tried to express love for Richard—she made him coffee in the morning and picked up his dry cleaning and cooked his dinner—but he always seemed dissatisfied. She didn't know what to do.

I explained to Richard and Suzanne that we all express and receive love in different ways. In a model (mentioned previously in Habit 60) popularized by Gary Chapman, author of *The Five Love Languages: The Secret to Love That*

Lasts, he identifies five categories of love expression: touch, gifts, acts of service, quality time, and verbal affirmation. While we respond to all five, each of us tends to have one preferred love language.

Therefore, if you express love primarily with touch, but your spouse really prefers gifts, it's as if you're speaking Italian but she only understands Chinese. You're speaking past each other. I mentioned my cat, who brings me dead birds and mice as a love offering. I thank her but explain that dead animals are not my love language!

I pointed out that Suzanne was using acts of service as an expression of love, but they weren't registering for Richard. As we explored further, Richard realized that he craved verbal affirmation (compliments, appreciation, words). I suggested to Suzanne that she lavish him over the next week with praise, both privately and publicly.

During their next session several weeks later, Richard beamed, "Now we're getting somewhere . . . I really do feel her love! She compliments me all the time now—even to my boss and my friends. I've never felt better. In fact, it kind of makes me want to be the man she believes me to be."

Once your mate tells you and others the qualities in you she prizes—your generosity, kindness, humor, compassion—you strive to increase these qualities. Your spouse's praise starts to expand your best nature . . . and *your* praise starts to expand *her* best nature.

Suzanne said, "It makes me happy to know that he's happy. And when he's feeling fulfilled, I can see that he's trying to make me happy. It feels like a win-win."

REFLECTION: How do you see your mate differently as you highlight his or her positive attributes?

HABIT 63

Only You

PROMPT: At least once a day

HABIT: Whisper and/or sign to your spouse your private code that says, "I love you." This is a sign that you both create and is known only to the two of you. It is a sign that you love each other "truly, madly, deeply."

PURPOSE: Drs. Charles and Elizabeth Schmitz, authors of *Building a Love That Lasts*, have been researching happily married couples in forty-six countries over the course of three decades. They believe that small daily moments are the foundation for a healthy marriage. Saying "I love you" in a heartfelt way is one of their recommended daily activities. Letting your spouse know that he's loved validates his place in your life. Also, when you express love daily, it helps keep your own heart open and flexible to the unexpected.

Having a *secret* sign (known only to the two of you) emphasizes intimacy and exclusivity. Whether it's verbal or physical, it should be appropriate to use in public so it can be used frequently. Since "love" is a word that is often used freely to describe feelings toward children, parents, friends, and even your favorite foods or movies, a private sign brings a unique, heightened quality to the expression.

It was the morning of Dan's surgery to remove a cancerous polyp. As you can imagine, it was a day fraught with many emotions. Dan was resting in a bed, already feeling relaxed from the initial sedative. I was doing my best to remain calm. As the cheerful anesthesiologist wheeled Dan to the operating room, they stopped at the "kissing corner" where I could say goodbye.

I might have thought of the others before me who stood at this corner sending their loved ones off to surgery with a kiss and a prayer for a positive outcome. I might have thought of the attendant, who must hear tearful "I love you's" at this corner multiple times a day.

But at that moment, only Dan and our secret sign was on my mind. I leaned over to kiss him and shared our secret symbol of love and connection.

My eyes filled with tears as they wheeled him off, but I was extremely grateful that we had a private symbol of love known only to the two of us.

REFLECTION: How has your childhood experience of love influenced how you express love now as an adult? When you were growing up, was love freely expressed?

HABIT 64

Magic

PROMPT: When your partner seems sad, stressed, or in need of an emotional pick-me-up

HABIT: Have a conversation with your spouse to help determine the magic words that make him or her feel the most loved and most valued. Once you know these individually tailored words that make your spouse's heart sing, go to your beloved and whisper them.

PURPOSE: This habit takes the inside track into the body, mind, heart, and soul of your spouse. Just as you might know exactly what button to push to really hurt her deeply (a button you should *not* be pushing), you need to know and use the words that especially touch her heart. By knowing her vulnerabilities, her deepest fears and concerns, you can discover the words that will soothe like a magical elixir of comforting love.

Once you learn her special words, use them frequently. These loving, healing words are custom designed to resonate. The words you use can either reassure her of your love and your commitment, or support her in a way that reduces stress.

When you take on the commitment of marriage, you also agree to help your spouse in both good times and bad times. When you see that she is struggling in some way, you can ignore her or assist her. Choosing to help her restore balance to her emotional world is known as "co-regulation." It is a common habit among happily married couples. When you use the magic words, you help your partner come to her calm center when she can't quite get there on her own.

Magic words are specifically different and yet universally the same for everyone:

- "You are my top priority."
- "I will be with you forever."

- "You have changed my life for the better."
- "I am completely happy with our life."
- "You are my hero."
- "You can depend on me no matter what."
- "I trust you."
- "I am here for you."

I have heard a man, whose mother died when he was young, respond to the words of his wife: "I am here for you, always." I have seen a woman, whose alcoholic father ignored her, react to the words of her husband: "I treasure you beyond all the riches in the world." I love helping couples find the words that will speak to their spouse, words that have a "zinger" quality in their power.

Sometimes finding the magic words can heal years of sorrow and pain. Reggie was a kind man who had grown up with the message that he was "no good." He had been a mediocre student in school, had never gone to college, but had lived a decent life working for a construction company.

Reggie had spent fifteen years in a marriage in which his wife berated him for not making enough money and not being ambitious. Deep down he believed her when she said he was a "loser." It was a message that was comfortably familiar even as it stripped him of his self-esteem.

When I introduced the idea of magic words to Reggie and his second wife, Tania, he knew what words he had always longed to hear: "Reggie, you are a fantastic husband and a wonderful man." Fortunately, Tania believed this so it was easy for her to tell this to her husband on a regular basis.

Tania knew that when she used these poignant words, not only was she conveying a healing message, she was doing everything in her power to make Reggie feel special. She told me that as she did so, she could feel her heart expand to bursting. This habit is a win–win for both partners.

REFLECTION: How do you feel when you give your lover the gift of words that heal his heart and lift his spirit?

CHAPTER 9

The Wind Beneath My Wings: Habits to Connect You in Spirit

In one way or another, every marriage has an impact on the world. Your combined total is greater than the sum of your parts. Amid all the millions of people in the world, the two of you found each other, and you have a purpose in your union.

When you see yourself as being part of a larger whole, you recognize the import of your togetherness. Perhaps you came together to create and/or raise children, to help each other heal, and to bring out the best in each other. Perhaps your destiny is about completing a project together.

Or maybe, without realizing it, by your example you are touching lives. This was true for Ned, an eighty-year-old widower who described his beloved wife as the kindest, gentlest, most lovely soul on the planet. They were deeply in love for more than forty years.

"Almost all of my condolence cards mentioned how happy we had been, how we were a light of love in the community," Ned said. "I didn't even know that people knew we were so happy. I didn't think it showed so much."

It showed because love is like the light shining from a lighthouse, emitting hope and happiness to others around you.

The habits in this section are about the "something more" between you. These habits will help you honor and recognize the larger energy between you and your spouse, an energy that is not only sacred and profound, but also timeless.

HABIT 65

Bless You

PROMPT: When you make the bed in the morning (or as you leave the bed in the morning)

HABIT: Wave your hand over the bed and think about how you're connected to your dear one. Say the words, "Beloved, may you be happy and healthy today. May you be safe from harm. I wish for you peace and happiness until you return for more rest."

PURPOSE: This habit is based on the Buddhist meditation practice called *Metta Bhavana*. *Metta* is Pali for "loving kindness" and *Bhavana* means "cultivation of." It's a five-stage practice of wishing loving kindness toward the self, toward a dear one, toward a stranger, toward an "enemy," and toward the world.

The neuroscientist Daniel Siegel, author of many books, including *Mindsight: The New Science of Personal Transformation*, points out that an intentional habit such as mentally giving goodwill to others has the power to change the architecture of your brain. You can train your brain to be more loving. With the habit of wishing your spouse well in the morning, you actively create a positive mental state, which in turn leads to a more harmonious marriage.

I learn a lot from my clients. Some of what I learn is as mundane as restaurant recommendations, books to read, and hotels to frequent. But I also learn about human nature and the amazing struggles through which people triumph.

Michael came to see me when his wife was going through chemotherapy treatment for breast cancer. He told me that he didn't have many friends to talk to and that his family was far away. Susanna, his wife of nine years, was his primary confidante.

But how could he tell her that he didn't find her attractive anymore without her hair, with her body wasting away? How could he tell her that he loved her beyond measure and that he was terrified of losing her? How could he tell her that he was exhausted by his caretaking duties and that he missed having her as a healthy wife?

Michael was brutally honest in our sessions. He found relief in being able to admit his unvarnished feelings—as if he was in a confessional. He now had a safe forum in which to reveal his struggles, one in which he was able to reflect on his deep and profound love for his wife.

He told me that almost every morning, while Susanna still slept, he tiptoed around the bed and stood beside her. He held his hand over her sleeping form and said the words, "I wish you good health and a long life with me."

"What a wonderful thing to do," I said. "That's the kind of loving habit that you could continue even after she gets well."

After a few months, when Susanna had finished her treatment, Michael and I ended our work together. About a year later, he sent me an e-mail to let me know that Susanna had just received a clean bill of health.

"One thing I still do," he wrote, "is my morning blessing for Susanna— whether she's in the bed or not. You were right—it helps me feel grateful for every day with her."

REFLECTION: If you spend a moment wishing your dear one well, how might it affect the energy that you take into your day?

Heaven on Earth

PROMPT: When you get into bed at night next to your beloved

HABIT: Touch your sweetheart on the arm and say, "Heavenly."

PURPOSE: Appreciation and gratitude feed your relationship and heighten your experience of happiness in your marriage. At the end of the day (literally), it is a healthy habit to experience gratitude for the great blessing and simple pleasure of sleeping next to your beloved.

The practice of gratitude actually shapes the neural structure in your brain in a way that strengthens your ability to experience more gratitude. The brain's capacity to change itself (neuroplasticity), means that when you intentionally exercise the gratitude area of your brain, it becomes stronger and more active. Likewise, when you stop using neurons of negativity, they eventually wither and weaken. Thus, going to sleep with gratitude for your spouse and the marital bed rather than bringing a mind full of worries to bed is a much better habit for your marriage and for your peace of mind.

Even if you happen to enter an empty bed, you can think it "heavenly" that you have a spouse whom you love and who will join you eventually. Let the habit of gratitude rest in your mind as you drift off to dreamland.

I am a native Texan, a girl who grew up thinking 50 degrees was freezing. After thirty years, I'm challenged by the northern climate. But when Dan gave me a heated mattress topper for Christmas one year, getting between the sheets became like sinking into a hot bath. It felt like heaven on earth.

When you let gratitude for your marriage sink into you, you'll find that it's habit-forming. The expression of gratitude is common to all happy marriages. As a nightly habit it not only puts you to sleep with a smile on your face, it also increases your capacity to bring gratitude into your daily communication with your spouse.

Isn't it a blessing to get into bed next to the warm body of someone who loves you, who accepts you, who has committed to sharing his life with you? Isn't it dreamy to lie next to someone who shows you every day that you matter to him? Isn't it a wonder to spoon a soul who connects to yours, who daily chooses to be with you?

With "heavenly" on your lips, you can go down for your long winter's nap, offering thanks for both the warm body and soul that graces your nights.

REFLECTION: Do you notice that you sleep better when you fill your mind with appreciation as you're drifting off?

HABIT 67

Teacher's Pet

PROMPT: When some behavior or characteristic of your partner is causing you to feel annoyed

HABIT: Imagine bowing respectfully to your beloved, recognizing that she is your teacher. Identify the deeper lesson, take note, and breathe into it. Say to yourself, "I am learning about _____" (patience, gratitude, compassion, love, change, acceptance, kindness, generosity, forgiveness). Thank you for this lesson."

PURPOSE: When you find yourself getting upset by something your partner does or doesn't do, this tool invites you to look for a deeper lesson. Sometimes what you dislike in your spouse is a quality mirroring what you dislike in yourself (such as tardiness, selfishness). Other times, it's a quality that you used to appreciate in your mate but is now causing you consternation (such as her spontaneity or devil-may-care attitude). Or perhaps your mate simply has a quality that you need to learn more about.

When you adopt the habit of treating your partner as your unlikely teacher, you will find life lessons open up to you every day.

Geraldine came to see me because she wanted to forgive her father, who had died five years previously, for being critical and abusive. However, in the course of our initial sessions, Geraldine spent most of the time complaining about her husband.

She told me that Marcus was irresponsible, flighty, and permissive. He never seemed to take things seriously, as if life were a big game. When I asked Geraldine what attracted her to Marcus some twelve years earlier, she said,

"Oh, it was his easy-going, lighthearted manner. He was like a breath of fresh air."

It's not uncommon for the very things that attracted you to your mate to turn into the things that most annoy you. The lighthearted man is now irresponsible. The playful party girl is now a flirtatious woman who ignites your jealousy. The ambitious woman is now a workaholic. The generous man now gives his time and money away.

As I listened to Geraldine, I asked for a recent example of how Marcus's easy-going attitude was affecting her negatively. "Well," she said, "when we were trying to sell our house last year, he just wasn't worried enough."

"Wasn't worried enough?" I asked, confused.

"He doesn't get how serious things are financially. We were so close to going into foreclosure but he just shrugged his shoulders and kept saying, 'It will be what it will be,'" she responded.

"Maybe he's your teacher about how to be more relaxed, more at peace regardless of your circumstances," I suggested.

Geraldine thought about that for a moment. I continued, "Ask yourself, what is Marcus teaching me . . . what can I learn from him? Do you really want his legacy to you to be that you learned to be more worried, more uptight, more stressed . . . or is there something more?"

She agreed to view Marcus as her teacher over the next few weeks. When she came back, she told me that she'd noticed from this perspective sometimes he really *could* help her be more lighthearted. She also noticed that sometimes the lesson seemed to be patience (learning how to not lose her cool when she found him annoying). Either way, by seeing him as her teacher, she began to relax in situations that ordinarily would cause her stress. Soon, she stopped complaining about her husband during counseling.

REFLECTION: In what ways are you a teacher for your spouse?

Toast of the Town

PROMPT: When you're having dinner out, just the two of you

HABIT: Clink your glasses together (even if it's just your water glasses) and toast to your relationship. Say, "To us" or "To our happy marriage." For extra emphasis, link your arms together as you might have on your wedding day.

PURPOSE: Honoring your formal relationship is a habit that will help provide and strengthen the special space that only the two of you share. Charlotte Kasl writes in *If the Buddha Married: Creating Enduring Relationships on a Spiritual Path* about what she calls the "us" space. She describes the "us" space as a form of alchemy in which the mixing of two substances transforms into something new. "I" and "you" becomes "us." This space needs to be regularly noticed, prioritized, and honored.

You might have offered a traditional pretzel-armed toast to your bride or groom on your wedding day, a special toast to the newly married "us" space, but how often since? Don't let a private drink together pass without recognition of your special relationship and your precious marriage.

There is something about a happy marriage that is palpable, tangible. You can essentially experience the love in the air around a happy couple. I will often suggest to couples who see me for counseling that they play a game called "I spy a happy couple." When in public, they watch couples around them and note which ones seem happy, identifying which characteristics reflect that happiness.

Usually my clients will report back things like, "Happy couples hold hands ... or they make eye contact with each other ... or they smile when they talk to each other ... or they kiss on the street." These, in fact, are characteristic habits of happily married couples, habits that keep individuals connected and energized.

My favorite happy couple story was reported back to me by my client Spencer.

"They were sitting next to me and Marjorie," he said. "They looked really happy and then—yes, I admit it, I was eavesdropping—I actually overheard them toast to each other." Spencer, who is very gregarious, said he leaned over to them and asked, "How many years have you been toasting to each other?"

The older gentleman responded enthusiastically, "We've been toasting to each other *every time* we dine out for the past fifty-five years. We're lucky, don't you think?" Lucky indeed. Of course, happy couples make their luck habit by habit, practiced regularly. Toast to your beloved and see how many years you begin to accumulate of happiness.

REFLECTION: What might happen in your life if you began to honor the *us* space on a regular basis?

HABIT 69

Honk

PROMPT: When your mate is upset and you want to support or encourage her

HABIT: Stand behind your beloved and place your hand firmly on her upper back, right between the shoulder blades. Then gently lean into her ear and *whisper* the words "Dear One, I hear you and I am here for you."

PURPOSE: John Gray, author of the classic *Men Are from Mars, Women Are from Venus*, speaks and writes eloquently about gender differences. He advises men that when women share their problems, they just want to be heard (not have their problems fixed). For women, when they're heard, the bonding hormone oxytocin is stimulated. Men may not have the same need to be listened to, but they do need to feel supported. They like to know that their mates stand beside them.

Thich Nhat Hanh, the wise and prolific Vietnamese Buddhist monk, suggests that the greatest gift we can ever give another is the gift of our full and undivided presence. He suggests using the phrase "Dear One, I am here for you" as a gift of love. Whispering these words adds an element of tenderness and intimacy.

Suzanne sat on my office couch with her hands crossed as if protecting her personal space. She said, "I just need a little support from you, that's all."

Hank looked dumbfounded. He shook his head. "But that's what I'm *trying* to do."

Tearfully, Suzanne replied, "Telling me that I work too much and should quit my job is *not* supporting me!"

Ah-ha. I started to get the sense that a common gender dynamic was taking place. Usually when women complain, they simply want to be heard. However, when women complain, men often want to fix the situation. They don't realize that all that's required of them is to listen, witness her feelings, and be a sympathetic presence.

If you've ever seen and heard a flock of geese flying in the air, you'll know it's one of nature's wonders. In V formation, the geese fly together as a tight, interdependent unit, with loud honks. Interestingly, the honk is a sign of encouragement from one goose to another to keep flying and stay the course. The lead goose at the head of the V creates an air draft from which the others can benefit. They take turns being at the lead. The honk is the ultimate cheerleader sound, meaning "I am here for you; I've got your back."

When Suzanne complained about her boss, her coworkers, or the stress of the day, she didn't want a solution from Hank. If she did, she would have asked for his advice. Nor did she want to be redirected or shut down. The support she desired was simply for Hank to listen to her and acknowledge her struggles.

As we worked on this goal in the session, and as Hank came to realize that it was his simple listening presence that mattered most to Suzanne, he was able to provide emotional support. As Suzanne realized she was not alone with her burden, she began to visibly relax. In the end, all she needed to hear was an encouraging "honk."

REFLECTION: How do you normally receive your partner's distress? What is stirred for you if you sit quietly with her struggles?

HABIT 70

Say Cheese

PROMPT: When you want to capture a wonderful moment with your spouse

HABIT: Wink at your loved one as if the wink were the shutter of a camera. Then proceed to hold the beautiful moment in your heart for ten seconds. Expand it, stretching the feeling as if you're pulling taffy. Let the moment sink into your being.

PURPOSE: With this habit, highlighted with a wink, you will be more able to savor your time as a couple. It is so easy for you to slog through the years, barely noticing what's going on right in front of you. Then when the kids are grown or a life chapter ends, you wonder where the years went.

When you let each special moment foster the growth of love and intimacy in your marriage, you begin a rewiring process in your brain. Rick Hanson, author of the bestselling book *Buddha's Brain: The Practical Neuroscience of Happiness, Love, and Wisdom*, talks extensively about the concept of "taking in the good." He claims that by consciously imprinting good experiences, (holding a good experience, expanding it, and mentally absorbing it into our bodies), we create new neural pathways of happiness.

This habit helps overcome our biological negativity bias: We are hard-wired to notice and remember things going wrong more than to notice things going right! However, by intentionally highlighting a pleasant moment and holding it in your awareness, positive neurons fire, thus wiring together, and bringing stronger traces of happiness into your implicit memory bank.

When Daniel and I first blended our family of five children and five pets, let's just say it was not an overwhelming success. I remember consulting books for stepfamilies and feeling crestfallen at the prognosis that most stepfamilies could expect to spend up to seven years in conflict. I stopped reading those books.

I began to get a glimmer of why second marriages have higher divorce rates even than first marriages—it often has to do with children and stepchildren and the loyalty binds that exist.

During our second summer of seven people under one roof, we took the kids to a lake house on a local New Hampshire pond for our first family vacation. It was a miraculous turning point. We enjoyed kayaks, a lake, popsicles, and s'mores by the fire pit. To our amazement, not only did everyone participate, but they actually enjoyed themselves. A stepsister helped a stepbrother make brownies. There was swimming. There was laughter.

On the third night, we sat around the dining room table on a screened-in porch, listening to loon calls on a still lake. Two adults and five kids played Cranium Family Edition. I recognized in that moment that the vacation was an unbelievably significant success. We were acting like a "normal" family. We were playing a game designed for families. We were *blending*.

I made eye contact with Daniel and we both smiled. I had a feeling of connection with him, a sense that "our bond will not be broken" and "we can get through any situation as long as we're together." He winked at me as if to say, "Look at us. This is a wonderful moment." And indeed it was.

REFLECTION: What beautiful moment today deserves a "wink" in your life?

HABIT 71

Wake Up

PROMPT: When you are having morning coffee or tea together

HABIT: Touch your spouse's arm and say, "I am so lucky to be married to you," or "I'm lucky that I found you in this wide world," or "I feel lucky to be spending my life with you."

PURPOSE: Make it a habit to wake up every day to the wonder of your lives together. As you wake up your body, use this habit to wake up to the miracle of spending your life with this beloved person! Out of all the billions of people on this planet, this is whom you are making a life with. Notice. Wake up. Be grateful.

Happy couples make their luck *and* happy couples are aware of their luck as well. They saturate their lives with gratitude. They recognize that they have a good thing going. So even if you feel a little frustrated with your mate at times, know that there is still much to savor.

Stating out loud that you feel lucky can become a self-fulfilling proposition. When you say that you're lucky, you start to feel lucky. When you feel lucky, you say so. Set this cycle of happiness in motion today so that you can treasure every precious moment.

And just like that, life changed. "It's cancer," the doctor told Daniel after a biopsy. I heard the news on a Friday and burst into tears. We were launched into a new world that included such scary things as a CT scan, a colonoscopy, surgery, an oncologist, and chemotherapy. I had a surreal sense of dissociation as if I were in a dream time warp.

But on that Friday when we heard the news, we sat on the precipice of the unknown. We didn't know the actual prognosis, whether the CT scan would show a body riddled with cancer or just one cancerous polyp. So we decided to spend the day at the beach watching the waves and searching for sea glass. All we knew was that for the moment we had each other.

Sitting with Daniel in a café, I found myself wondering if I would be a widow anytime soon. I looked around at the couples casually sipping their lattes. Didn't they know that this moment, this time over a coffee was precious? Didn't they know that this moment was all we had?

I turned my attention to this man across from me, a man who was my husband in sickness and in health. I touched his hand and murmured that no matter what, I felt incredibly lucky to be his wife.

REFLECTION: How would your relationship change if your spouse only had a few months to live?

State of the Union

PROMPT: At least once a season, (use the solstice and equinox as reminders) when you have at least ten minutes to sit down quietly together

HABIT: Rate your current relationship on a scale of one to ten, with one being "I'm on the brink of divorce" to ten being "honeymoon heaven." First, get your number in your head and then share it simultaneously with each other. Reflect on the numbers and discuss, if necessary, what you think is required to move the number higher. State what you are personally willing to do to help improve the number, not just what you wish your partner would do. Hold this brief discussion lovingly with a willingness to look at your own behaviors as well as your partner's.

PURPOSE: Just as good businesses develop the habit of regular performance reviews, so too do happy marriages. When you are willing to look at "what is" and how to improve it, you knit yourselves closer together as a couple. It takes a certain amount of courage to engage each other in honest reflection and to voice what's going right and what needs a little tweaking. Just the act of taking this review seriously will begin to increase your marital intimacy.

Your numbers are diagnostic of the health of your relationship. It's important to understand how happy (or how unhappy) your spouse is. If your number is significantly higher than that of your spouse, ask him what you can do to help bring his number higher. As with any good diagnosis, once you know what you're dealing with, you can start the treatment.

I've been using the "State of the Union" habit with couples for years to help them assess their relationship. I'm always amazed that most couples are within one number of each other. That said, the numbers tend to be on the medium to low side. The most common assessment I see in my practice is usually a five or a six. (They *are* in couples counseling, after all.)

One noteworthy exception stands out in my mind. A couple married for thirty-one years came to see me at the wife's insistence. I asked them to do this "State of the Union" relationship assessment. To my surprise the husband held up an eight and the wife held up a one. It turns out she had brought him to session to tell him that she wanted a divorce.

As we explored her dissatisfaction in the relationship, she pointed out that they hadn't had sex for years, they barely spoke, they never touched, and they weren't kind to each other. Their children were long gone and there seemed no reason to continue living as roommates.

"We haven't been above a five in my mind for at least twenty years," she added. "Too bad we didn't try to get help then."

Unlike these two, couples who use this tool regularly can track the ups and downs of their relationship and of each other's satisfaction in the marriage. Like early detection in health care, knowing the truth and intervening where necessary offers your marriage its best chance of good health and long-term survival.

REFLECTION: What price might you pay by staying "too busy" to assess the state of your union?

HABIT 73

Cave Time

PROMPT: When your spouse seems irritable, or specifically says that he needs some time alone

HABIT: Suggest that your spouse take some time for himself for restoration. Agree on a time (thirty minutes, an hour) when you will reconvene.

PURPOSE: Everyone needs time to him- or herself, but for some people the need is greater. Typically men and introverts need lots of time alone to replenish and refuel. It's nothing personal, just a natural need.

In a happy marriage, you should develop the habit of letting your spouse have the space he needs to be healthy and relaxed. All marriages require times of togetherness and times of space. It's vital to the health of your marriage that you allow your spouse the undisturbed alone time that he needs. After his cave time, he'll be more willing and able to connect with you.

John Gray points out in his book *Why Mars and Venus Collide: Improving Relationships by Understanding How Men and Women Cope Differently with Stress* that men especially require time alone to disengage and forget their problems. A stressful day lowers men's testosterone levels, making them irritable, anxious, and tired. Private downtime raises their hormone levels, thus reducing their stress and enabling them to engage socially.

Marsha was a gregarious, fun-loving gal who worked from home in IT sales. She connected with people on the phone and on the Internet all day long, but by the time her beloved Zack came home from work, she was starved for real face-to-face connection. She eagerly and enthusiastically practiced the "Puppy Love" reunion hug habit (Habit 7). Then she was ready to hear all about Zack's day and tell him about hers.

The problem was that Zack was extremely drained when he came home at night. As a pediatrician, he had spent the day dealing with crying infants, sick toddlers, anxious teens, and worried parents. When he arrived home, he wanted to sit in front of the news and zone out.

Marsha felt abandoned when Zack zoned out so quickly after coming home. Emotionally, she couldn't understand his need for private time. Zack couldn't understand Marsha's need to chat. And so they couldn't quite honor each other's requirements in a respectful way. The end result was that no one got what they wanted.

Before they worked with me, Zack would come home exhausted but, not wanting to hurt Marsha's feelings, would try to talk to her. However, he listened to her chatting only half heartedly. His cursory answers seemed to Marsha like rejection. Feeling misunderstood, he would get angry that she couldn't empathize with his fatigue. They often went to bed mad at each other.

I suggested that Zack spend forty-five minutes completely alone when he returned from work (after the reunion hug, of course.) Then, after dinner, he would spend up to forty-five minutes alone with Marsha, giving her his undivided attention. In other words, they could both have their needs met, just not at the same time.

The next week, they both expressed delight with the arrangement. Zack had his private time to relax and unwind and Marsha was able to offer this gift freely because she knew that he'd be more able to connect with her afterward. Most important, they were no longer going to bed angry.

REFLECTION: Be open to the possibility that when you grant the needs of your spouse, she or he will be open to granting your needs as well.

HABIT 74

My Guy

PROMPT: Whenever you're introducing your spouse to other people, or even when you're around others and wish to refer to your spouse

HABIT: Own your connection to each other with a strong term of affection and make it public. Find the words that you're comfortable with to emphasize your adoration: my best half, my beloved husband, my true love, my beautiful bride, my dear one, my cherished partner, etc.

PURPOSE: When you develop the habit of bestowing titles of endearment on your partner, several important things happen. First, you signal to others that you consider your relationship special. Second, you communicate to your dear one that she is, indeed, important and cherished by you. Last, you create a couples language that engenders solid feelings of connectedness and intimacy.

The words that you use with your spouse are happiness indicators in your marriage. Happy marriages tend to overflow into public expressions of your relationship: expressions of togetherness (terms of endearment), partnership (holding hands, praise, and compliments), and love (hugging and kissing). When you use strong terms of endearment with each other in public, you and your spouse strengthen your bond of trust, and show one another that you will be there through thick and thin.

It's awkward enough to attend your own college reunions: the small talk, the comparisons, and the assortment of hazy memories. But, consider the awkwardness of attending your spouse's college reunion.

That was how Stacey felt about going to Carl's tenth. She said angrily, "It's not like it was fun for me, if you know what I mean."

Carl rolled his eyes upwards and said, "Here we go again . . ."

"What, specifically, was the problem?" I asked.

Stacey jumped in. "Every single time he introduced me, he would say . . . 'and this is Stacey.' Not once did he admit that I was his *wife*." She looked down into her lap. "I could have been his sister, a friend . . . a hired escort—anyone."

Carl snorted. "That's not how it was. I just think labels are silly. Why should it matter?"

I explained to Carl that it *did* matter. Happy couples have the habit of prizing each other in public. Most important, it mattered to Stacey. That, in and of itself, should have been enough of a reason to motivate his behavior.

Stacey felt about as important as used chewing gum, but Carl remained unconvinced. He left my office stating that if she was that insecure, a silly label wouldn't make any difference.

Stacey and Carl never returned to my office but if I were to make a guess, I'd say that Stacey was no longer Carl's wife.

REFLECTION: Is there any reason not to proclaim to the world that you are in a committed relationship?

HABIT 75

Hawaiian Luau

PROMPT: When you're getting ready for bed

HABIT: Look yourself in the eye in a mirror and say the following phrases three times: "I love you. I'm sorry. Please forgive me. Thank you." Say it like a chant.

PURPOSE: These phrases are the core of the ancient Hawaiian Huna practice known as *Ho'o pono pono*. Traditionally it was considered a mental cleansing practice of reconciliation and restoration. Often performed by a priest or elder, the ritual consisted of repeating these phrases and symbolically letting go, followed by a feast.

The modern version of this practice is to repeat the phrases like a chant. The result is a healing experience that puts relationships right and facilitates self-love. When you make it a habit to say these words of love, forgiveness, and gratitude, you will feel cleansed.

In the book *The Things You Would Have Said: The Chance to Say What You Always Wanted Them to Know*, Jackie Hooper collects letters of ordinary people saying the things they wished they could have said to loved ones while they had the chance. The common themes in these letters are exactly the words of *Ho'o pono pono*. Say these words regularly and with intention and you will feel an emotional freedom. The result is that your marriage—and your well-being—will flourish.

Note: Keep a Post-it note on your mirror with the phrases so that you'll remember to use the habit.

Although it might seem awkward or even pointless to repeat the set of *Ho'o pono pono* phrases, I have seen it work wonders. I have seen a husband having difficulty with an ex-wife use the phrases and watch the contentiousness between them dissolve. I have seen a woman who struggled with body image issues—to the point that she wasn't comfortable having sex with her husband—learn to love herself and feel comfortable in her own skin.

However, my favorite *Ho'o pono pono* example is that of sixty-five-year-old Nancy. When Nancy came to see me, she was holding decades of guilt. In her forties, she had cheated on her husband of fifteen years. Even though they had both gone on to remarry happily, she couldn't find it in her heart to forgive herself.

Cheating had gone against everything she'd ever believed. At the time, she had been in an emotionally cold marriage and so when she met Greg and fell in love, she didn't know what to do. Greg had swept her off her feet, and soon she had discovered that she was capable of dark deceit. She was still plagued by the image of her first husband's face when he discovered that she was having an affair.

I suggested to Nancy who typically avoided looking herself in the eye that she try the "Hawaiian Luau" habit.

Over the course of the next two months, Nancy was willing to be open to the process of change. Making eye contact with herself in the mirror, she repeated the words faithfully morning after morning, even when she didn't believe they were true. "I love you. I'm sorry. Please forgive me. Thank you." And over this time, her heart began to heal. She started to feel lighter, freer, released from a burden. She couldn't really describe what shifted for her other than gaining a feeling that she deserved love.

That feeling translated to a deeper ability to connect with her current husband, Greg. Forgiveness of yourself translates to love of others. If you've ever struggled with self-acceptance and self-compassion, the time is *now* to make peace. Your marriage depends on it.

REFLECTION: Has there been a time in your life when you were overflowing with self-love?

CONCLUSION

Safe Harbor

I heard a glass clink hard on the table beside us. A woman sighed heavily and leaned away from the man across from her, saying, "I just don't think this will work out. Why should we waste the evening pretending? I'm sorry . . . I'm sure you're a nice guy but I just don't find you attractive."

I looked away, trying not to eavesdrop but unable to help myself. I heard chairs scraping as she stood and put on her coat. She turned to go, saying, "It was nice to meet you and I hope you find the right woman."

I was fascinated by this drama of a failed match. Saturday night was just beginning, but two lonely hearts were going home alone. The guy threw some bills on the table and left crestfallen, his shoulders hunched.

We all want to be matched, paired, and mated. We all want to feel close, connected, and wanted. These human desires are so natural that they're woven into your DNA. It's your biological—and emotional—goal to fall in love and make a commitment to each other.

You not only want to be happy in your union, you deserve to be. Your marriage is too precious to let it dissolve into loneliness or anger.

I once listened to an elderly gentleman tell me that he had been married for forty-six fabulous years. "Every year gets better," he said with a smile. "In fact, it took the first decade to understand each other, the next to accept each other, and the third to heal each other's emotional wounds. Now, well, we just love each other with the brakes off."

Ahhh. Love each other with the brakes off . . . every day. You don't need to wait forty years to do this. Nor do you have to assume that only newlyweds love with this deep passion. All you need to do is recharge and reconnect every day, knowing that your marriage is a tremendous gift.

Daniel and I hope that you will thread the habits in this book through your days to enrich your connection, increase your intimacy, and sustain your love through all the circumstances of your life. Together you can be stronger, wiser, and happier than you ever imagined.

Bibliography

Buber, Martin. *I and Thou.* Translated by Ronald Gregor Smith. (New York, NY: Scribner Classics, 2000).

Bush, Ashley Davis. *Shortcuts to Inner Peace: 70 Simple Paths to Everyday Serenity.* (New York, NY: Berkley Books, 2011).

Chapman, Gary. *The Five Love Languages: The Secret to Love That Lasts.* (Chicago, IL: Northfield, 1996).

Davis, Michele Weiner. *The Sex-Starved Marriage: Boosting Your Marriage Libido, A Couple's Guide.* (New York, NY: Simon & Schuster, 2003).

Doherty, William J., PhD. *Take Back Your Marriage: Sticking Together in a World That Pulls Us Apart.* (New York, NY: Guilford, 2003).

Edmond, Mishabae, and John Running. *The Joy of Partner Yoga.* (New York, NY: Sterling, 2004).

Feinstein, David, Donna Eden, Gary Craig, and Michael J. Bowen. *The Promise of Energy Psychology: Revolutionary Tools for Dramatic Personal Change.* (New York, NY: Penguin, 2005).

Ferguson, Bill. *How to Heal a Painful Relationship: And If Necessary, Part As Friends*, 2nd ed. (Houston, TX: Return to the Heart, 1999).

Ford, Arielle. *Wabi Sabi Love: The Ancient Art of Finding Perfect Love in Imperfect Relationships.* (New York, NY: HarperOne, 2012).

Goldsmith, Barton. *Emotional Fitness for Couples: 10 Minutes a Day to a Better Relationship.* (Oakland, CA: New Harbinger, 2005).

————. *Emotional Fitness for Intimacy: Sweeten and Deepen Your Love in Only 10 Minutes a Day.* (Oakland, CA: New Harbinger, 2009).

Gottman, John M. *The Seven Principles for Making Marriage Work: A Practical Guide from the Country's Foremost Relationship Expert.* (New York, NY: Three Rivers, 2000).

Gray, John, PhD. *Men Are from Mars, Women Are from Venus: The Classic Guide to Understanding the Opposite Sex.* (New York, NY: Harper, 2004).

————. *Why Mars and Venus Collide: Improving Relationships by Understanding How Men and Women Cope Differently with Stress.* (New York, NY: Harper, 2008).

Hanh, Thich Nhat. *True Love: A Practice for Awakening the Heart.* (Boston, MA: Shambhala, 1997).

Hanson, Rick, PhD. *Buddha's Brain: The Practical Neuroscience of Happiness, Love & Wisdom.* With Richard Mendius, MD (Oakland, CA: New Harbinger, 2010).

Hatch, Claire. *Save Your Marriage: Get Rid of Your Resentment.* (Amazon Digital Services, Inc., 2011).

Hendricks, Gay, and Kathlyn Hendricks. *Conscious Loving: The Journey to Co-Commitment*. (New York, NY: Bantam, 1992).

Hendrix, Harville. *Getting the Love You Want: A Guide for Couples, 20th Anniversary Edition*. (New York, NY: Henry Holt, 2007).

Hunt, Lyn. *Massage in a Relationship: Effective Body Massage Techniques Made Easy, Reduces Stress, Improves Relaxation and Communication, and Deepens Your Relationship*. (Amazon Digital Services, Inc., 2012).

Johnson, Sue. *Hold Me Tight: Seven Conversations for a Lifetime of Love*. (New York, NY: Little, Brown, 2008).

Kasl, Charlotte Sophia, PhD. *If the Buddha Married: Creating Enduring Relationships on a Spiritual Path*. (New York, NY: Penguin, 2001).

Kawamura, Yasuko. *You Knead Me: How to Massage Your Partner's Neck in 10 Easy Ways*. (Amazon Digital Services, Inc., 2012).

Kelly, Matthew. *The Seven Levels of Intimacy: The Art of Loving and the Joy of Being Loved*. (New York, NY: Touchstone, 2005).

Lager, Susan. *Become Relationship Smart Without a Lifetime of Therapy*. (CreateSpace, 2013).

Lerner, Harriet, PhD. *Marriage Rules: A Manual for the Married and the Coupled Up*. (New York, NY: Gotham, 2012).

Levine, Stephen, and Ondrea Levine. *Embracing the Beloved: Relationship as a Path of Awakening*. (New York, NY: Anchor, 1996).

Love, Patricia, and Steven Stosny. *How to Improve Your Marriage Without Talking about It.* (New York, NY: Three Rivers, 2008).

Lucas, Marsha, PhD. *Rewire Your Brain for Love: Creating Vibrant Relationships Using the Science of Mindfulness.* (New York, NY: Hay House, 2012).

Masters, Robert Augustus. *Transformation Through Intimacy: The Journey Toward Awakened Monogamy*, rev. ed. (Berkeley, CA: North Atlantic, 2012).

Perel, Esther. *Mating in Captivity: Unlocking Erotic Intelligence.* (New York, NY: Harper Perennial, 2007).

Real, Terrence. *The New Rules of Marriage: What You Need to Know to Make Love Work.* (New York, NY: Ballantine, 2008).

Ringer, Judy. *Unlikely Teachers: Finding the Hidden Gifts in Daily Conflict.* (Portsmouth, NH: OnePointPress, 2006).

Runkel, Hal Edward. *ScreamFree Marriage: Calming Down, Growing Up, and Getting Closer.* With Jenny Runkel. (New York, NY: Crown Archetype, 2011).

Schmitz, Charles D., and Elizabeth A. Schmitz. *Building a Love That Lasts: The Seven Surprising Secrets of Successful Marriage.* (San Francisco, CA: Jossey-Bass, 2008).

Siegel, Daniel J. *Mindsight: The New Science of Personal Transformation.* (New York, NY: Bantam, 2011).

Simpkins, C. Alexander, and Annellen Simpkins. *The Dao of Neuroscience: Combining Eastern and Western Principles for Optimal Therapeutic Change.* (New York, NY: W. W. Norton, 2010).

Solomon, Marion, and Stan Tatkin. *Love and War in Intimate Relationships: Connection, Disconnection, and Mutual Regulation in Couple Therapy.* (New York, NY: W. W. Norton, 2011).

Tatkin, Stan. *Wired for Love: How Understanding Your Partner's Brain and Attachment Style Can Help You Defuse Conflict and Build a Secure Relationship.* (Oakland, CA: New Harbinger, 2012).

Acknowledgments

Having John Willig, of Literary Services, Inc., to represent us has been a source of tremendous joy. Even during trying economic times, John believed in this project from the beginning. He saw the potential and the need for this book and made a match with the perfect publishing house. We couldn't ask for a finer literary agent!

Working with the folks at Adams Media, beginning with Victoria Sandbrook and including every member of the team, has been a total delight. Peter Archer, our dedicated editor, provided fresh direction, clear guidance, and creative solutions to push this project to its highest potential. It has been an invigorating process to collaborate with such a visionary publishing house.

We are extremely grateful to the clients who invite us on the intimate journey of growth and healing. They teach, inspire, and motivate us to be better people. Having the honor of working in the field of psychotherapy is truly a gift.

We thank our families, especially our five children, who have been hearing about the contents—and watching the progress—of this book for several years.

Finally, we want to extend particular gratitude to you, the reader, for investing the time and energy into improving your marriage. It takes courage to insist on an intimate connection and we applaud your efforts! Thank you for letting us help you on the journey.

About the Authors

Ashley Davis Bush, LCSW, is a psychotherapist in private practice with over twenty-five years of experience helping people live richer, deeper lives. She is the author of three other self-help books: *Shortcuts to Inner Peace: 70 Simple Paths to Everyday Serenity* (Berkley Books, 2011), *Claim Your Inner Grown-up: 4 Essential Steps to Authentic Adulthood* (Putnam, 2001), and *Transcending Loss: Understanding the Lifelong Impact of Grief and How to Make It Meaningful* (Berkley Books, 1997).

Ashley is a regular blogger for the Huffington Post and an accomplished singer/actress.

Daniel Arthur Bush, PhD, began his career in the academic world of anthropology. He made a midlife career change to the mental-health field when he began managing Ashley's psychotherapy practice and eventually became trained as a mental-health counselor.

Ashley and Daniel together have recovered from their first marriages, blended a family, learned healthy communication skills, and developed these habits to help them stay intimate, connected, and in love every day. They consider their marriage to be one of the greatest blessings in their lives.

Index